Insights
for Today

Third Edition

Reading For Today SERIES, BOOK 2

LORRAINE C. SMITH

Adelphi University

NANCY NICI MARE

English Language Institute
Queens College
The City University of New York

THOMSON
HEINLE

Australia • Canada • Mexico • Singapore • United Kingdom • United States

THOMSON

™

HEINLE

Insights for Today, Third Edition
Lorraine C. Smith and Nancy Nici Mare

Publisher, Adult and Academic ESL: *James W. Brown*
Senior Acquisitions Editor: *Sherrise Roehr*
Director of Development: *Anita Raducanu*
Development Editor: *Sarah Barnicle*
Senior Production Editor: *Maryellen E. Killeen*
Senior Marketing Manager: *Charlotte Sturdy*
Director, Global ESL Training & Development:
Evelyn Nelson
Senior Print Buyer: *Mary Beth Hennebury*

Contributing Writer: *Barbara Gaffney*
Compositor: *Parkwood Composition Service*
Project Manager: *Hockett Editorial Service*
Photo Researcher: *Susan Van Etten*
Photography Manager: *Sheri Blaney*
Illustrator: *Glenn Reid*
Cover Designer: *Ha Ngyuen*
Text Designer: *Carole Rollins*
Printer: *Edwards Brothers*

Printed in the United States of America
1 2 3 4 5 6 7 8 9 10   06 05 04 03

For more information contact Heinle, 25 Thomson Place,
Boston, Massachusetts 02210 USA, or you can visit our
Internet site at http://www.heinle.com

For permission to use material from this text or product
contact us:
Tel   1-800-730-2214
Fax   1-800-730-2215
Web   www.thomsonrights.com

Library of Congress Control Number   2003107155

ISBN   0-88377-111-X
ISE ISBN   1413000762

To Steven

CREDITS

Photographs

p. 1, © David Young-Wolff/PhotoEdit

p. 2, Courtesy, Bob Wjcieszack

p. 4, Courtesy, Don Seabrook

p. 11, Courtesy, Marlene Graham

p. 19, © A. Ramey/PhotoEdit

p. 21, © David Barron/Oxygen Group

p. 26, © AFP/CORBIS

p. 29, © James A. Sugar/CORBIS

p. 37, © SW Production/Index Stock Imagery

p. 38, © Mary Kate Denny/PhotoEdit

p. 40, Courtesy, Abelone Glahn

p. 51, © Myrleen Ferguson Cate/PhotoEdit

p. 60, © Myrleen Ferguson Cate/PhotoEdit

p. 62, © David Young-Wolff/PhotoEdit

p. 75, © James Harvey/Index Stock Imagery

p. 85, © Lester Lefkowitz/CORBIS

p. 86, © Steve Starr/Index Stock Imagery

p. 89, © Michael Newman/PhotoEdit

p. 100,© Michael Newman/PhotoEdit

p. 102, © Michael Keller/CORBIS

p. 109, © Jim Bourg/Getty Images

p. 111, © AP/Wide World

p. 120, © Roger Ressmeyer/CORBIS

p. 122, © Reuters NewMedia, Inc./CORBIS

p. 129, © Myrleen Ferguson Cate/PhotoEdit

p. 130, © Joseph Tenga

p. 132, © Jennie Woodcock; Reflections Photo Library/CORBIS

p. 146, © Paul Frankian/Index Stock Imagery

p. 153, © Dana White/PhotoEdit

p. 155, © photolibrary.com pty/Index Stock Imagery

p. 157, © PhotoDisc/Getty

p. 168, © Tom Stewart/CORBIS

p. 179, © Vander Zwalm Dan/CORBIS SYGMA

p. 180, Photograph by Joseph Tenga, Courtesy of the United States Committee for UNICEF

p. 182, © Craig Hammell/CORBIS

p. 194, © CORBIS

p. 201, © Bettmann/CORBIS

p. 203, © Royalty-Free/CORBIS

p. 215, © Bettmann/CORBIS

p. 225, Courtesy, NASA

p. 241, © Harry Brown, 2003, The Do-It Homestead, Utah

p. 266, © Reuters NewMedia, Inc./CORBIS

p. 270, © Joseph Tenga

CONTENTS

Unit	Chapter and Title	Reading Skills Focus	Structure Focus	Follow-up Activities Skills Focus
CNN® Video Report and Internet Topics				
Unit 1 **Today's Travelers** *Page 1*	Chapter 1 **A Family Sees America Together** *Page 2* **Courtney's Texas** *Page 11*	• Preview visuals and use titles and pre-reading questions to activate prior knowledge • Understand True/False, Multiple Choice, Short Answer questions • Skim reading for main idea • Scan for information • Recall information, make inferences, draw conclusions • Choose accurate dictionary definitions • Use context clues to understand vocabulary • Read and understand maps	• Identify parts of speech in context: nouns and verbs • Use the singular and plural nouns, and the simple present tense.	• *Listening-Speaking:* Express opinions • *Writing:* Make a plan; Write an opinion paragraph; Write a journal entry
• **CNN® Video Report:** Volunteer Vacations • **Internet Search:** Volunteering and Habitat for Humanity *Page 56*	Chapter 2 **Volunteer Vacations** *Page 19* **Who Volunteers?** *Page 29*	• Use graphic organizers to organize answers and activate prior knowledge • Understand True/False, Multiple Choice, Short Answer questions • Skim reading for main idea • Scan for information and use a chart to record ideas • Use context clues to understand vocabulary • Choose accurate dictionary definitions • Make inferences • Assert opinions	• Identify parts of speech in context: nouns and verbs • Recognize the suffix: *-tion* • Use singular and plural nouns, and affirmative or negative forms of the simple present tense.	• *Listening-Speaking:* Share information; Make a list of interview questions in pairs; Listen and share opinions • *Writing:* Write an opinion paragraph supporting with reasons and examples; Write a journal entry
Unit 2 **Family Life** *Page 37*	Chapter 3 **How Alike Are Identical Twins?** *Page 38* **Diary of a Triplet Father** *Page 51*	• Use background knowledge to understand reading • Understand True/False, Multiple Choice, Short Answer questions • Skim reading for main idea • Scan for information • Use a graphic organizer to take notes • Use context clues to understand vocabulary • Make inferences and draw conclusions • Choose accurate dictionary definitions	• Identify parts of speech in context: adjectives and nouns; verbs and nouns • Recognize the suffix: *-ness* • Use the affirmative or negative forms of the simple present tense; Use singular or plural nouns	• *Listening-Speaking:* Develop interview questions and conduct an interview • *Writing:* Write a descriptive paragraph; Write positive and negative reasons; Write a journal entry expressing likes and dislikes;
• **CNN® Video Report:** Raising Triplets • **Internet Search:** Identical Triplets *Page 84*	Chapter 4 **The Search for Happiness through Adoption** *Page 60* **Diary of an Adoptive Mother** *Page 74*	• Preview visuals and answer prereading questions to activate prior knowledge • Understand True/False, Multiple Choice, Short Answer questions • Skim reading for main idea • Scan for information and take notes in a chart • Use context clues to understand vocabulary • Choose accurate dictionary definitions • Make inferences; draw conclusions • Read, understand, and use statistics	• Identify parts of speech in context: nouns and verbs • Recognize the suffix: *-ion* • Use the affirmative or negative of the simple present tense; Use singular or plural nouns	• *Listening:* Listen and note opinions of others • *Writing:* Write a dialogue; Write a letter; Write an opinion paragraph; Use imagination to write a journal entry

SKILLS

Unit	Chapter and Title	Reading Skills Focus	Structure Focus	Follow-up Activities Skills Focus
CNN® Video Report and Internet Topics				
Unit 3 **Technology in Our Everyday Lives** *Page 85*	Chapter 5 **Laptops in the Classroom** *Page 86* **Banking at Home** *Page 100*	• Preview photos to activate prior knowledge • Understand True/False, Multiple Choice, Short Answer questions • Skim reading for main idea • Scan for information and take notes in a flowchart • Use context clues to understand vocabulary • Choose accurate dictionary definitions • Make inferences; draw conclusions • Make predictions • Understand content area vocabulary about *technology*	• Identify parts of speech in context: nouns and verbs • Use the singular and plural nouns, and affirmative or negative forms of the simple present tense.	• *Listening-Speaking:* Report experiences to class about a banking or computer experience; Compare lists of advantages and disadvantages with class • *Writing:* Write and compare lists; Write a journal entry justifying an opinion
• **CNN® Video Report:** Dean Kamen and Segway • **Internet Search:** Young Inventors and Segway *Page 128*	Chapter 6 **A New Way to Go** *Page 109* **Young Inventors** *Page 120*	• Use visuals to make predictions • Understand T/F, Multiple Choice, Short Answer Questions • Skim reading for main idea • Read for supporting details • Scan for information • Use a chart to take notes • Make inferences • Use context clues to understand vocabulary • Choose accurate dictionary definitions • Understand content area vocabulary about *inventions*	• Identify parts of speech in context: nouns and verbs • Recognize the suffix: *-ion* • Use the affirmative or negative form of the simple present tense.	• *Listening-Speaking:* Create an invention with a group and report on it with visual aids • *Writing:* Write a descriptive paragraph; Write a journal entry about a proposed invention
Unit 4 **Healthy Living** *Page 129*	Chapter 7 **The Dangers of Secondhand Smoke** *Page 130* **Smoking Facts and Figures** *Page 145*	• Preview chapter through photos and prereading questions • Understand True/False, Multiple Choice, Short Answer questions • Skim reading for main idea • Scan for information • Take notes in flowchart • Use context clues to understand vocabulary • Choose dictionary definitions • Make inferences • Read and understand statistics • Understand content area vocabulary about *smoking* and *health*	• Identify parts of speech in context: nouns vs. verbs; nouns vs. adjectives • Recognize the suffix : *-ness* • Use the singular and plural nouns, and affirmative or negative forms of the simple present tense.	• *Listening-Speaking:* Role plays; Small group problem-solving; Discuss and design advertising • *Writing:* Write laws about smoking; Write copy for an advertising agency; Write a comparison paragraph about laws; Write a journal entry justifying an opinion or argument
• **CNN® Video Report:** Ten Healthy Foods • **Internet Search:** Health and Nutrition *Page 178*	Chapter 8 **A Healthy Diet for Everyone** *Page 153* **Why Do I Eat When I'm Not Hungry?** *Page 168*	• Preview photos with prereading questions • Understand True/False, Multiple Choice, Short Answer questions • Skim for main idea • Scan for information • Take notes in flowchart • Use context clues to understand vocabulary • Choose dictionary definitions • Make inferences • Draw conclusions • Understand content area vocabulary about *nutrition* and *health*	• Identify parts of speech in context: nouns and verbs • Recognize the suffix : *-ment* • Use the affirmative or negative of the simple present tense.	• *Listening-Speaking:* Discuss steps to a healthy lifestyle • *Writing:* Write a list of ways to stay healthy; Write a descriptive journal entry

Skills ix

Unit	Chapter and Title	Reading Skills Focus	Structure Focus	Follow-up Activities Skills Focus
CNN® Video Report and Internet Topics				
Unit 5 **International Scientists** *Page 179*	Chapter 9 **Alfred Nobel: A Man of Peace** *Page 180* **Choosing Nobel Prize Winners** *Page 194*	• Preview photos with prereading questions • Understand True/False, Multiple Choice, Short Answer questions • Skim for main ideas • Scan for information using a graphic organizer to take notes • Use context clues to understand vocabulary • Make inferences • Draw conclusions • Choose dictionary definitions • Understand content area vocabulary about *Alfred Nobel* and *the Nobel Peace Prize*	• Identify parts of speech in context: nouns and verbs • Recognize the suffixes: *-ion, -ation,* and *-ment* • Use singular and plural nouns, affirmative and negative verb forms and simple present tense appropriately in sentences	• *Listening-Speaking:* Work with a committee to create a plan for a new Nobel category and vote as a class • *Writing:* Write instructions; Write a biography; Write a support paper arguing in favor of someone; Make a list from research at the library; Write a descriptive journal entry
• **CNN® Video Report:** Albert Einstein • **Internet Search:** Nobel Prize and Famous Scientists *Page 224*	Chapter 10 **Marie Curie: A Twentieth Century Woman** *Page 201* **Irene Curie** *Page 215*	• Preview photos with prereading questions • Understand True/False, Multiple Choice, Short Answer questions • Skim for main ideas • Scan for information • Take notes on a timeline and explain notes • Use context clues to understand vocabulary • Make inferences; draw conclusions • Choose dictionary definitions • Understand content area vocabulary about *Marie Curie, Irene Curie,* and *their scientific experiments*	• Identify parts of speech in context: nouns, verbs, and adjectives • Recognize nouns by the suffix: *-ance, —ence,* or *-ness* • Use singular and plural nouns, affirmative and negative verb forms and simple present tense appropriately in sentences	• *Listening-Speaking:* Create a list with a partner; Listen for information; Compare ideas; Discuss • *Writing:* Fill out a chart with ideas from a partner discussion; Write a descriptive paragraph or explanatory paragraph; Write a brief comparison; Write a process paragraph; Write a biography and/or autobiography; Write a journal entry;
Unit 6 **The Earth's Resources and Dangers** *Page 225*	Chapter 11 **Oil as an Important World Resource** *Page 226* **The DO IT Homestead** *Page 241*	• Generate a list to activate background knowledge • View diagram and fill out flowchart with information • Understand True/False, Multiple Choice, Short Answer questions • Use a flowchart to take notes • Skim for main idea • Scan for information using a graphic organizer to take notes • Use context clues to understand vocabulary about *oil production* • Make inferences; draw conclusions • Choose dictionary definitions • Read, understand, and extract information from diagrams, a map, and a numerical table	• Identify parts of speech in context: nouns, verbs, and adjectives • Recognize nouns by the suffix: *-tion* • Use singular and plural nouns, affirmative and negative verb forms and simple present tense appropriately in sentences	• *Listening-Speaking:* Create a list with a partner; Listen for information; Compare ideas • *Writing:* Fill out a chart with ideas from a partner discussion; Write a descriptive paragraph; Write a process paragraph; Write a journal entry

Unit	Chapter and Title	Reading Skills Focus	Structure Focus	Follow-up Activities Skills Focus
CNN® Video Report and Internet Topics				
• **CNN® Video Report:** Solar Roofs • **Internet Search:** Alternative Energy and Solar Roofs Initiative *Page 278*	Chapter 12 **How Earthquakes Happen** *Page 251* **A Survivor's Story** *Page 266*	• Use title to understand main idea • View photos with prereading questions • Understand True/False, Multiple Choice, Short Answer questions • Use a flowchart to take notes • Skim for main idea • Scan for information using a graphic organizer to take notes • Use context clues to understand vocabulary about earthquakes • Make inferences; draw conclusions • Choose dictionary definitions • Read and draw information from a diagram, a map, and a numerical table	• Identify parts of speech in context: nouns, verbs, and adjectives • Recognize nouns by the suffix: *-ment* • Use singular and plural nouns and affirmative and negative verb forms appropriately in sentences	• *Listening-Speaking:* Interview someone; Give reasons and explanations; Create a list with a classmate; Generate an action plan with a team • *Writing:* Write a composition from interview notes; Write a list of instructions; Write a journal entry describing a real or imaginary experience
	Index of Key Words and Phrases *Page 279* **Skills Index** *Page 281*			

PREFACE

Insights for Today, Third Edition is a reading skills text intended for high-beginning English-as-a-second or foreign-language (ESL/EFL) students. The topics in this text are fresh and timely, and the book has a strong global focus.

Insights for Today is one in a series of five reading skills texts. The complete series has been designed to meet the needs of students from the beginning to the advanced levels and includes the following:

- *Themes for Today*   beginning
- *Insights for Today*   high beginning
- *Issues for Today*   intermediate
- *Concepts for Today*   high intermediate
- *Topics for Today*   advanced

Insights for Today, Third Edition provides students with essential practice in the types of reading skills they will need in an academic environment. It requires students to not only read text, but also extract basic information from various forms of charts, graphs, illustrations, and photographs. Beginning-level students are rarely exposed to this type of reading material. Furthermore, the students are given the opportunity to speak and write about their own experiences, country, and culture in English, and to compare them with those of the United States and other countries. This text has real-life activities that give students specific tasks to complete outside the classroom. These tasks provide students with opportunities to practice reading, writing, speaking, and listening to English in the real world. Thus, all four skills are incorporated into each chapter.

Insights for Today, Third Edition has been designed for flexible use by teachers and students. The text consists of six units. Each unit contains two chapters that deal with related subjects. At the same time, though, each chapter is entirely separate in content from the other chapter contained in that unit. This gives the instructor the option of either completing entire units or choosing individual chapters as a focus in class. If the teacher chooses to do both chapters, there is a discussion question at the end of the unit which ties the two related topics together. Furthermore, although the chapters are organized by level of difficulty, the teacher and students may choose to work with the chapters out of order, depending on available time and the interests of the class. In like manner, the activities and exercises in each chapter have been organized to flow from general comprehension, including main ideas and supporting details, through vocabulary in context to critical thinking skills. However, the teacher may choose to work on certain exercises out of order, depending on time and on the students' abilities.

The opening illustrations and the prereading preparation before each reading help activate the students' background knowledge of the topic and encourage the students to think about the ideas, facts, and vocabulary that will be presented in the passage. In fact, discussing illustrations in class helps lower-level students visualize what they are going to read about and gives them cues for the new vocabulary they will encounter. The exercises which follow the reading passage are intended to develop and improve reading proficiency, including the ability to learn new vocabulary from context, and comprehension of English sentence structure. The activities give students the opportunity to master useful vocabulary encountered in the articles through discussion and group work and lead the students through comprehension of main ideas and specific information.

Lower-level language students need considerable visual reinforcement of ideas and vocabulary. This is why this text contains so many illustrations. It is also why so many of the follow-up activities enable students to manipulate the information in the text and supplemental information. In fact, the teacher may want the students to do the charts and lists in the activities on the board.

Much of the vocabulary is repeated throughout the exercises and activities in any given chapter. Experience has shown that low level students especially need a lot of exposure to the same vocabulary and word forms. Repetition of vocabulary in varied contexts helps the students not only understand the new vocabulary better, but also helps them remember it.

A student-centered approach will facilitate student learning. Wherever possible, students should be actively engaged through pair work or small group work. Except for the actual process of reading, students can engage in almost all of the activities and exercises with a partner or in a small group. By working with others, students have more opportunities to interact in English. Student group work also frees the teacher to circulate throughout the class and give more individual attention to students than would be possible if the teacher directed most of the classwork from the front of the room.

As the students work through *Insights for Today* they will learn and improve reading skills, and develop confidence in their growing English proficiency skills. At the same time, the teacher will be able to observe their steady progress toward skillful, independent reading.

New to the Third Edition

While *Insights for Today* retains the overall format of the second edition, the authors have made several significant changes. The third edition contains two new chapters: "Volunteer Vacations," a chapter about an alternative way to spend vacation, and "A New Way to Go," a chapter about the Segway and other inventions. These additions provide students with extensive reading practice about twenty-first century topics.

Insights for Today contains an enhanced Prereading Preparation section, which provides thoughtful, motivating illustrations and activities. The third edition includes improved graphics art and photos, which are designed to facilitate students' understanding of the text they relate to. The Skimming and Scanning Exercise includes a main idea activity as well as outlines, charts, and flowcharts, depending on each reading and the type of information it contains. This design takes into account students' different learning and organizational styles. The Think About It section contains questions to develop students' critical thinking skills. Dictionary Skills provides students with the opportunity to improve their ability to use an English dictionary, and to become less dependent on a bilingual dictionary. Topics for Discussion and Writing includes questions for journal writing, providing even more opportunities for students to incorporate writing as a natural part of reading. Word Search activities and Crossword Puzzles offer a review of the vocabulary encountered in each chapter.

In addition to the new chapters, the third edition is now accompanied by a CNN® video composed of video clips to complement the theme of one of the chapters in each unit. At the end of each unit, video activities accompany the video to assist students in their viewing comprehension.

Also new to *Insights for Today, Third Edition* are Internet Activities designed to encourage students with school or home access to the Internet to learn more about a topic they read about in their text.

All of these revisions and enhancements to *Insights for Today, Third Edition* have been designed to help students improve their reading skills, to reinforce vocabulary encountered, to encourage interest in the topics students examine, and to develop confidence as they work through the text. All of these skills are presented to prepare students for academic work and the technical world of information they are about to encounter.

INTRODUCTION

How to Use This Book

Every chapter in this book consists of the following:

Prereading Preparation
Reading Passages
Fact-Finding Exercise
Skimming and Scanning Exercise
Reading Analysis
Think About it
Dictionary Skills
Word Forms
Another Look
Follow-up Activities
Topics for Discussion and Writing
Word Search
Crossword Puzzle
Grammar Cloze Quiz

At the end of each unit there is a discussion section, which ties together the related topics in the two chapters for that unit, as well as CNN® video and Internet activities. An Index of Key Words and Phrases and a Skills Index are at the end of the book.

The format of each chapter in the book is consistent. Although each chapter can be done entirely in class, some exercises may be assigned for homework. This, of course, depends on the individual teacher's preference, as well as the availability of class time.

Prereading Preparation

This prereading activity is designed to activate students' background knowledge, stimulate student interest and provide preliminary vocabulary for the passage itself. The importance of prereading preparation should not be underestimated. Studies have shown the positive effect of prereading preparation in motivating student interest and in enhancing reading comprehension. In fact, prereading discussion in general and discussion of visuals has been shown to be very effective in improving reading comprehension. Students need to spend time describing and discussing the illustrations as well as the prereading questions. Furthermore, the students should try to relate the topic to their own experience, and try to predict what they are going to read about. The teacher can facilitate the students' discussions by writing their guesses and predictions about the reading on the blackboard. This procedure helps motivate student interest by providing a reason for reading. This process also helps the teacher evaluate the students' knowledge of the content they are about to read so they can be provided with additional background information where needed. The students can review their predictions after they have read the passage in order to check their predictions for accuracy. The important point to keep in mind is not whether the students' guesses are correct, but rather that they think about the reading beforehand and formulate predictions about the text. Once the students have considered the title, accompanying illustration, and prereading questions, they are ready to read the passage.

The Reading Passage

As the students read the passage for the first time, they should be encouraged to read *ideas*. In English, ideas are groups of words in sentences and in paragraphs, not in individual words. After the students read the passage to themselves, the teacher may want to read the passage aloud to the students. At lower levels, students are very eager to learn pronunciation, and feel that this practice is helpful to them. Moreover, reading aloud provides the students with an appropriate model for pronunciation and intonation, and helps them hear how words are grouped together by meaning.

Students may wish to maintain individual records of their reading rate. They can keep track of the time it takes them to read a passage for the first time, then record the length of time it takes them to read it a second time. Students should be encouraged to read text from beginning to end without stopping, and to read at a steady pace, reading words in meaningful groups or phrases. Once they have established a base time for reading, they can work to improve their reading rate as they progress through the book.

Fact-Finding Exercise

After the first reading, students will have a general idea of the information in the passage. The purpose of the Fact-Finding exercise is to check the students' general comprehension. The students will read the True/False statements and check whether they are true or false. If the statement is false, the students will go back to the passage and find the line(s) which contain the correct information. They will then rewrite the statement so that it becomes true. This activity can be done individually or in pairs. Doing this exercise in pairs allows the students to discuss their answers with their partner, and to explain their reasons for deciding if a statement is true or false. When all of the students have finished the exercise, they can report their answers to the class.

Skimming and Scanning Exercise

Students need practice with the two skills of skimming a reading for the main idea, and scanning it for specific information. Before doing this exercise, the teacher should make it clear to the students the difference in purpose between skimming and scanning, and explain that each activity requires a different way to read. When skimming, it will be helpful for the students to keep the title in mind, and to ask themselves, "What is this reading telling me about?" In the first part of the activity, students are asked to read the passage a second time in order to understand the main idea of the reading. When preparing students for this exercise, the teacher should encourage the students to ignore unknown vocabulary, and to focus on understanding the most important idea of the reading. When going over the exercise, the teacher should discuss with the students why the other answers are incorrect. In the second part of the activity, students should be instructed to read the passage carefully again and to pay attention to details. They will complete the chart or outline, or answer the questions on specific information in the passage, and compare their answers with a classmate's. The pairs of students can then refer back to the passage and check their answers. When the class is finished, one or more students can complete the chart or outline on the board so the students can check and discuss their answers as a whole group.

Reading Analysis

At this point, the students have read the passage at least three times, and should be familiar with the main idea and the content of the reading. The Reading Analysis exercise gives students an opportunity to learn new vocabulary from context. In this exercise, the students will read each question and answer it. This exercise requires the students to think about the meanings of words and phrases, the structure of sentences and paragraphs, and the relationships of ideas to each other. This exercise is very effective when done in pairs or groups. It may also be done individually, but working together gives the students an excellent opportunity to discuss possible answers.

Think About It

The goal of the exercise is for the students to go beyond the reading itself to form their own ideas and opinions on aspects of the topic discussed. The students reflect on the content of the reading, and think about the implications of the information they have read. The students can work on these questions as an individual writing exercise or orally as a small-group discussion activity. In this activity, students are encouraged to use the vocabulary they have been learning.

Dictionary Skills

The entries in this section have been taken from *The Newbury House Dictionary*. This exercise provides students with much needed practice in using an English-English dictionary and in selecting the appropriate dictionary entry for an unknown word. The students are given a dictionary entry for one of the words in the text. A sentence containing the unknown word is provided below the entry. The students read the entry and select the appropriate definition, given the context provided. Students need to understand that this is not always a clear process; some entries are similar. They should be encouraged to carefully read all of the possible definitions in the context in which the word is given, and to consider which meaning makes the most sense, given the context. After selecting the appropriate entry, the students read two or three sentences, and choose which one conveys the meaning of the definition selected. The students can work in pairs on this exercise and report back to the class. They should be prepared to justify their choice.

Word Forms

Students often know one form of a word but do not recognize it in a different form. This exercise gives the students practice in seeing the noun, verb, adjective, and adverb forms of vocabulary which appear in the readings. As an introduction to the word form exercises in this book, it is recommended that the teacher first review parts of speech, especially verbs, nouns, adjectives, and adverbs. Teachers should point out each word form's position in a sentence. Students will develop a sense for which part of speech is missing in a given sentence. Teachers should also point out clues to tense and number, and whether an idea is affirmative or negative. Each section has its own instructions, depending on the particular pattern that is being introduced. For example, in the section containing words which take *-tion* in the noun form, the teacher can explain that in this exercise the student will look at the verb and noun forms of two types of words that use the suffix *-tion* in their noun form. (1) Some words simply add *-tion* to the verb: suggest/sugges*tion*; if the word ends in *e*, the *e* is dropped first: produc*e*/produc*tion*; (2) other words can drop the final *e* and add *-ation*: examine/examin*ation*. The teacher can use the examples given in the directions for each chapter's Word Form section and make up sentences to see that the students understand the exercise. This exercise is very effective when done in pairs because students can discuss their answers. After students have a working knowledge of this type of exercise, it can be assigned for homework.

Another Look

The second reading in the chapters provides another point of view, or an additional topic, related to the main reading. The students should focus on general comprehension, on relating this reading to the primary reading, and on considering the ideas and information as they engage in the Follow-up Activities and Topics for Discussion and Writing. It is not necessary to spend additional time on unfamiliar vocabulary, unless it interferes with the students' ability to respond to the questions.

Follow-up Activities

This section contains various activities appropriate to the information in the passages. Some activities are designed for pair and small group work. Students are encouraged to use the information and vocabulary from the passages both orally and in writing. The teacher may also use these questions and activities as home or in-class assignments. The Follow-Up Activities help the students interact with the real world because many exercises require the students to go outside the classroom to get specific information. They are not limited to speaking, reading, or learning in the classroom.

Topics for Discussion and Writing

This section provides ideas or questions for the students to think about and/or work on alone, in pairs, or in small groups. Students are encouraged to use the information and vocabulary from the passages both orally and in their writing. The writing assignments may be done entirely in class, begun in class and finished at home, or done at home. The last activity in this section is a journal-writing assignment that provides the students with an opportunity to reflect on the topic in the chapter and respond to it in some personal way. Students should be encouraged to keep a journal and to write in it regularly. The students' journal writing may be purely personal, or the students may choose to have the teacher read them. If the teacher reads them, the journals should be considered a free writing activity, and should be responded to rather than corrected.

Word Search

The Word Search gives students an exercise in word recognition. Students often enjoy this type of word puzzle because it is challenging, yet not too difficult. The Word Search activity contains several words from the main reading. The words appear in every direction: left to right, right to left, top to bottom, bottom to top, diagonally, forward, and backward. It may be done individually first, and then students can compare their work. Students usually like doing such puzzles; even weaker students experience success with this type of word puzzle. Students can complete the Word Search activity on their own or with a partner after they have completed an in-class assignment, and may be waiting for the rest of their classmates to finish their work.

Crossword Puzzle

The Crossword Puzzle in each chapter is based on the vocabulary used in that chapter. Students can go over the puzzle orally if pronunciation practice with letters is needed. The teacher can have the students spell out their answers in addition to pronouncing the word itself. Students invariably enjoy doing crossword puzzles. They are a fun way to reinforce the vocabulary presented in the various exercises in each chapter, and require students to pay attention to correct spelling. At the same time, the students need to connect the meaning of a word and think of the word itself. If the teacher prefers, student can do the Crossword Puzzle on their own or with a partner in their free time, or after they have completed an in-class assignment and are waiting for the rest of their classmates to finish.

Grammar Cloze Quiz

The Grammar Cloze Quizzes in each chapter serve as a final review of the primary reading. These quizzes are guided and vary throughout the text. In each Grammar Cloze Quiz, certain types of words are missing. These words may be articles, prepositions, verbs, or pronouns. Students can work on the quizzes alone, and then compare their answers with a partner, or they may do them alone and the teacher can check their answers.

Unit Discussion

This section contains one or two questions which help the students connect the related topics in the two chapters for that unit. The questions may be discussed in class or assigned as written homework.

CNN® Video and Internet Activities

At the end of each unit are optional activities designed to accompany one of the topics presented in each unit. The authentic CNN® videos were chosen to continue concepts presented in the readings, to reinforce vocabulary learned, and to encourage individual interest as well as group discussion. The optional Internet activities provided encourage students to explore information learned in *Insights for Today* through the technology available to them at school, in the library, or at home.

Index of Key Words and Phrases

This section contains words and phrases from all the chapters for easy reference. It is located after the last chapter. The Index of Key Words and Phrases may be useful to students to help them locate words they need or wish to review.

ACKNOWLEDGMENTS

We are grateful to everyone at Heinle, especially to Sherrise Roehr for her continued support, to Sarah Barnicle for her keen eye and untiring efforts, and to Maryellen Killeen for her hard work. Special thanks also go to Rachel Youngman of Hockett Editorial Service for her diligence. As always, we are appreciative of the ongoing encouragement from our family and friends.

L.C.S. and N.N.M.

TODAY'S TRAVELERS

1

A Family Sees America Together

Prereading Preparation

1. Look at the photograph of the family. What are they planning to do?

   a. take a weekend trip

   b. take a short vacation

   c. take a long vacation

2. Look at the title of the chapter. Where does the family plan to travel?

   a. Canada

   b. the United States

   c. Mexico

3. How long will their trip be? (Write a specific amount of time.)

   _____

4. How many miles will they travel? (Write a specific number of miles.)

   _____

A Family Sees America Together

The Graham family of Wichita, Kansas, did something very unusual last year. Mr. and Mrs. Graham did not go to work, and their children did not go to school. Instead, Craig and Marlene Graham and their children, Courtney, 12, and Collier, 4, traveled together in a van and drove across America for a whole year.

First, Craig and Marlene sold their businesses. Craig had a real estate business, and Marlene owned a small newspaper. Then they sold their large house. Finally, Courtney said goodbye to her classmates, and their dream trip was ready to begin. The Graham family started their trip on July 4, Independence Day. They visited big cities and small towns in all 50 states. They also visited the birthplaces of all the United States' presidents. They wanted to visit many interesting places, parks, and zoos in the United States, but they also wanted to meet the American people. The Grahams had many wonderful experiences. Many people were very friendly and helpful to them. Some people invited the Graham family to stay in their homes with them. Everyone signed their "guest book."

Every day, Marlene wrote reports about her family's trip. She described the family's daily experiences, where they went, and what they did. Courtney kept a journal of her life on the road. Marlene and Courtney put their writing on their website. Schoolchildren from all over the United States followed the Graham family's trip by using computers at home and in school. Some children wrote letters to the Graham family. American newspapers published stories about the Grahams, and people interviewed the family on television shows.

At the end of the year, Craig said that they all had a wonderful trip. Courtney said that she missed her friends at school, but also enjoyed the trip very much. The Grahams traveled a total of 54,944 miles. They returned home on the same date that they left: July 4. They plan to write a book about their travels to describe everything they learned about their country and the American people.

Fact-Finding Exercise

Read the passage once. Then read the following statements. Check whether they are True or False. If a statement is false, rewrite the statement so that it is true. Then go back to the passage and find the line that supports your answer.

1. ____ True ____ False   The Graham family traveled across America together in a van.

_____

2. ____ True ____ False   The Graham family did not meet many friendly, helpful people.

_____

3. ____ True ____ False   Craig and Collier wrote reports about their trip every day.

_____

4. ____ True ____ False   The Graham family had a wonderful trip.

_____

5. ____ True ____ False   Schoolchildren used computers to follow the Grahams' trip.

_____

Skimming and Scanning Exercise

PART 1

Skim through the passage. Then read the following statements. Choose the one that is the correct main idea of the reading.

a. The Graham family liked to drive very far in a large van.

b. The Graham family left their home and their jobs to travel across the United States for one year.

c. The Graham family wanted to leave Kansas to find a new place to live.

PART 2

Scan the passage. Work with a partner to complete the chart below about the Graham family's trip.

	Craig	Marlene	Courtney	Collier
Is this person an adult or a child?				
What did he or she do before the trip?				
What did he or she do during the trip?				
What did he or she say after the trip?		✕		✕

Read each question carefully. Circle the letter or the number of the correct answer.

1. The Graham family of **Wichita, Kansas** did something very **unusual** last year.
   a. **Wichita** is a
      1. city
      2. state
   b. **Kansas** is a
      1. city
      2. state
   c. **Unusual** means
      1. special, different
      2. ordinary, common

2. Mr. and Mrs. Graham did not go to work, and their children did not go to school. **Instead,** Craig and Marlene Graham and their two children drove across America **for a whole year.**
   a. **Instead** means
      1. in place of
      2. in addition to
   b. Complete the following sentence correctly.
      Maria did not want to learn to play the violin. **Instead,**
      1. she learned to play the piano
      2. she tried to play the violin
   c. **A whole year** is
      1. less than one year
      2. exactly one year
      3. more than one year

3. The Graham family visited big cities and small towns **in all 50 states.** How many states are there in the United States?

   a. Less than 50

   b. Exactly 50

   c. More than 50

4. They also visited the **birthplaces** of all the United States' Presidents.

   Your **birthplace** is

   a. the place where you live

   b. the place where your children were born

   c. the place where you were born

5. Courtney **kept a journal** of her life **on the road.**

   a. **Kept a journal** means

      1. wrote in a journal

      2. saved a journal

      3. read a journal

   b. **On the road** means

      1. lying in the street

      2. traveling

      3. sitting inside a car

D. *Think* About It

Read the following questions and think about the answers. Write your answers below each question. Then, compare your answers with those of your classmates.

1. American newspapers published stories about the Grahams, and people interviewed the family on television shows. Why did people want to know about the Grahams' trip?

   _____

   _____

   _____

2. Courtney Graham did not go to school for a whole year. Do you think her teachers were angry? Why or why not?

   _____

   _____

   _____

E. DICTIONARY SKILLS

Read the dictionary entry for each word, and think about the context of the sentence. Write the number of the appropriate definition on the line next to the word. Then choose the sentence with the correct answer.

1.
> **dream** *n.* **1** a fantasy experienced while asleep: *The child has bad dreams.* **2** s.t. hoped for, *(syn.)* an **aspiration:** *She has a dream about being an engineer.* **3** a beautiful person or thing: *They're building their dream house. See:***American** Dream; daydream.

The Graham family had a **dream** to travel across America together.

a. **dream:**

[C]—Countable (noun) [U]—Uncountable (noun) / s.o.—someone s.t.—something / *(syn.)*—synonym *n.*—noun   *v.*—verb /

b. 1. The Graham family had fantasies in their sleep about traveling across America.

   2. The Graham family were all beautiful people.

   3. The Graham family hoped to travel across America.

2. | **experience** *n.* **1** [U] an event, a happening: *Our visit to Alaska was a pleasant experience.* **2** [U] understanding gained through doing s.t.: *She has years of experience in teaching.* |

The Grahams had many wonderful **experiences** during their year on the road.

a. **experience:** _____

b. 1. The one-year trip across America was a wonderful event for the Grahams.

   2. The one-year trip across America was a wonderful understanding for the Grahams.

3. | **own** *v.* **1** to have as property, *(syn.)* to **possess:** *She owns a bookstore.* **2** to admit, acknowledge: *The judge owned that the juror was biased.* **3** phrasal v.insep. **to own up to s.t.:** to confess, admit to s.t.: *The little boy finally owned up to the fact that he ate all the cookies.* |

Marlene **owned** a small newspaper. She sold her business before the trip began.

a. **own:** _____

b. 1. Marlene possessed a small newspaper business. She sold her property before the trip began.

   2. Marlene acknowledged a small newspaper business before the trip.

F. Word Forms

In English, the noun form and the verb form of some words are the same, for example, *walk (v.), walk (n.).* Read each sentence. Write the correct form of the word on the left. Then circle (*v.*) if you are using a verb or (*n.*) if you are using a noun. **Write all the verbs in the simple past tense. The nouns may be singular or plural.**

interview

1. a. John _____ the governor of Kansas last night.
   (v., n.)

   b. John did several _____ with the governor last
   year, too. *(v., n.)*

plan

2. a. Martha and Jim made some exciting _____ for
   their vacation last summer. *(v., n.)*

   b. They _____ to visit the county's capital and a
   (v., n.)
   national park, and they had a wonderful time.

report

3. a. The weather _____ for yesterday included rain
   (v., n.)
   and strong winds.

   b. The weatherman _____ that many trees fell down
   (v., n.)
   and some houses were damaged.

visit

4. a. I have made a few _____ to the City Museum of
   Art. *(v., n.)*

   b. I _____ the Museum four times last winter.
   (v., n.)

Read Courtney's journal entry describing her family's visit to Texas, and look at the map of Texas. Then answer the questions which follow.

Courtney's Texas—Big History, Big Cities, Big Hearts

Texas is a big state. The first town we visited was El Paso. Two other neat towns were San Antonio and Austin. Austin is the capital city. It's very modern, very technology-oriented, and is really growing. We visited the capitol building there. Photographers from the ABC station in Austin met us at the capitol and took some shots of us looking around.

After Austin, we headed on to San Antonio. We got to stay at the Marriott on the Riverwalk. The manager heard about our trip and let us stay for a night. That was so nice! They even gave us cheese and fruit. Wow! We felt so welcome.

In San Antonio, we also got to see the Alamo. Hard to believe this is where Davy Crockett died. All those people in the Battle of the Alamo were so brave, especially since many of them weren't Texans, just other guys trying to help the Texans gain their freedom from Mexico. Davy Crockett and his fighters were from Tennessee. Inside the Alamo, you can see some of the actual guns that were used. A television crew from the ABC station in San Antonio did a story with us, too. It was kind of neat to be filmed at the Alamo.

Of course, you've heard of other big cities in Texas like Houston. We had planned on spending some time there with a family we had met over the Internet, but we didn't make it to Houston because we were trying to get back on schedule.

There are a lot of neat places in Texas. This is a really cool state. But then if you're from Texas, you already know that.

1. Courtney wrote that Texas has a big history, big cities, and big hearts.
   a. Texas has a big history means that
      1. the history of Texas is very interesting
      2. the history of Texas is very large

   b. Texas has big hearts means that
      1. Texans are very friendly people
      2. Texans have hearts that are very large

2. The Graham family had two interesting experiences in Austin, Texas. What were they?

   _____

   _____

3. What did you learn about Texas after reading Courtney's journal? Check the information that you read about.

   _____ a.   Texas is a very big state.

   _____ b.   Texas has many mountains.

   _____ c.   Texas used to be part of Mexico.

   _____ d.   Texas has very cold weather.

   _____ e.   Davy Crockett was not from Texas.

   _____ f.   The Alamo was a famous battle in Texan history.

   _____ g.   Texans like to travel.

4. Does Courtney like Texas?
   a. Yes
   b. No

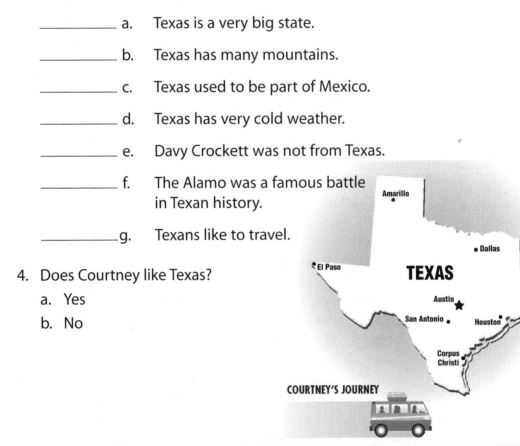

1. The Grahams' trip took one year, and they traveled 54,944 miles. Check the guesses you made on page 2. Which student in the class guessed the length and distance of the trip the most accurately?

2. The Graham family began their trip on July 4. They traveled to the 50 states in the following order: Kansas, Nebraska, Iowa, Wisconsin, Minnesota, North Dakota, South Dakota, Wyoming, Montana, Alaska, Washington, Oregon, Idaho, Utah, Colorado, Nevada, California, Hawaii, Arizona, New Mexico, Texas, Oklahoma, Arkansas, Louisiana, Mississippi, Alabama, Florida, Georgia, South Carolina, North Carolina, Tennessee, Kentucky, West Virginia, Virginia, Maryland, Delaware, Pennsylvania, New Jersey, New York, Connecticut, Rhode Island, Massachusetts, Vermont, New Hampshire, Maine, Ohio, Indiana, Michigan, Illinois, Missouri. They ended their trip on July 4, one year later in Kansas.

   a. Look at the map of the United States, and then trace their route on the map below.

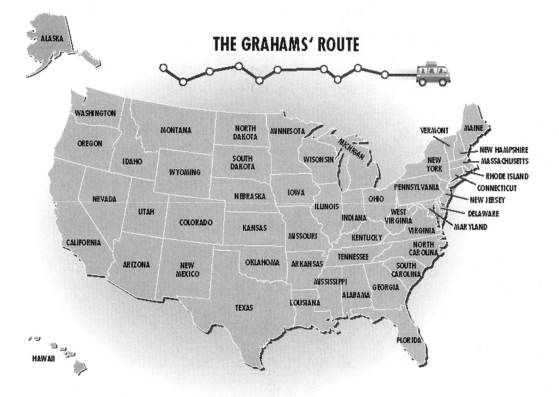

THE GRAHAMS' ROUTE

b. Read the list below. Check the reasons you think the Graham family followed this route.

_____ 1. because of the weather

_____ 2. because they liked some states better than other states

_____ 3. because many of the states were next to each other

_____ 4. because they wanted to visit their family

_____ 5. because this route was the most direct

_____ 6. because they got lost several times

2. Go to www.usatrip.com and visit the Grahams' website. What are they doing now?

I. *Topics* FOR *Discussion* AND *Writing*

1. Pretend that you will take a trip in the United States. Write a paragraph. Describe where you will go. What will you visit there?

2. Do you think it is a good idea to travel in a van with your family? Why is it a good idea? Why is it a bad idea?

3. **Write in your journal.** Describe a trip that you took alone or with your family. Did you enjoy it? Why or why not?

J. Word Search

Read the words listed below. Find them in the puzzle and circle them. They may be written in any direction.

dreams	Internet	planning	unusual
experiences	interview	report	visit
instead	journal	travels	works

```
E  X  P  E  R  I  E  N  C  E  S  I  J  E  W
F  K  L  M  H  Q  N  P  D  S  N  Q  N  F  O
L  O  A  O  J  U  V  T  A  T  M  S  P  A  R
U  X  N  O  A  O  G  O  E  G  N  A  Z  Q  K
J  O  N  S  C  A  U  R  T  R  A  V  E  L  S
B  O  I  L  R  N  N  R  S  I  V  E  D  R  N
V  E  N  N  U  E  Y  C  N  M  S  I  W  I  D
E  Q  G  S  T  P  P  X  I  A  U  I  E  D  L
G  A  U  N  E  X  T  O  D  Z  L  F  V  W  C
V  A  P  A  S  H  N  W  R  X  K  E  E  T  P
L  V  R  Y  J  R  O  Q  O  T  B  F  X  T  X
```

Read the clues on the next page. Write the answers in the correct spaces in the puzzle.

Crossword Puzzle Clues

Across Clues

4. Our class ends _____ 2 o'clock.
6. Newspapers _____, or print, information.
7. Not typical; not usual
8. We _____; she has
10. You write your personal experiences in a _____.
12. The city or town you were born in is your _____.
17. Real estate is a kind of _____.
19. John isn't here _____. He'll be here in a few minutes.
21. People ask other people questions in an _____ for television or the newspaper.
25. A _____ is something you hope for all your life.
27. Pleasant; agreeable
28. The past tense of **put**

Down Clues

1. The opposite of **down**
2. The other students in your class are your _____.
3. He _____ a teacher in our school.
5. To take a trip
7. **I, me; we, _____**
9. The opposite of **yes**
11. John wrote his name from left to right _____ the top of his paper.
13. Courtney Graham didn't study in school. _____, she studied during her trip.
14. I will meet you _____ 3:30.
15. An _____ is something that happens to you.
16. I wear glasses, _____ Debbie doesn't.
18. The _____ is a system of computers around the world.
20. The opposite of **no**
22. I am going _____ the store.
23. A large automobile
24. You and I
26. **I, _____; he, him**

First, read the story below. Then use the following pronouns to fill in the blanks. You may use each pronoun more than once.

she	they
her	their

Every day, Marlene wrote reports about _____ family's trip.
(1)

_____ described the family's daily experiences, where
(2)

_____ went, and what they did. Courtney kept a journal of
(3)

_____ life on the road. Marlene and Courtney put
(4)

_____ writing on the Internet. At the end of the year, Craig said
(5)

that _____ all had a wonderful trip. Courtney missed
(6)

_____ friends at school, but _____ also enjoyed the
(7)   (8)

trip very much. The Grahams traveled a total of 54,944 miles.

_____ returned home on the same date that they left. The family
(9)

plans to write a book about _____ travels.
(10)

2

Volunteer Vacations

Prereading Preparation

1. What are volunteers?

   _____

2. What kinds of work do volunteers do? Work in a small group. Use the diagram below to help you organize your answers. When you are finished, share your answers with the class.

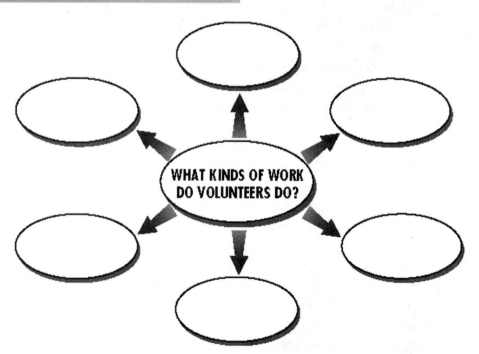

WHAT KINDS OF WORK DO VOLUNTEERS DO?

3. Look at the photograph on page 19. What are these people doing?

   _____

4. Who are they building the house for? What do you think?

   _____

5. What are some reasons that people volunteer to help others?

   _____

Volunteer Vacations

1   Everyone enjoys taking a vacation. A vacation is fun and relaxing. Some people like to go to the beach and swim. Other people go to the mountains or visit another country. Many other people use their vacation time for another reason. What do they do? They take a volunteer vacation to help other people.

5   Volunteers are people who do something, but they receive no money for it. They do this because they want to be helpful to people in need. Many organizations give volunteers a chance to help others.

     Habitat for Humanity is one of these organizations. Habitat for Humanity is an organization of volunteers who build homes for the poor. The most famous

10   volunteer is former U.S. President Jimmy Carter, who won the Nobel Prize for Peace. Habitat for Humanity volunteers don't need any special skills. They just need to be in good health. Volunteers build homes in the United States, but they also construct homes all over the world, in places such as Honduras, Fiji, and Ethiopia. Volunteers pay for their own trips. For example, a two-week trip to

15   Honduras, Fiji, or Ethiopia is about $1,200.

     A second volunteer organization is called Earthwatch. Earthwatch gets many volunteers to help scientists do research in many places around the world. For example, volunteers may study endangered animals such as manatees in Florida. Most of the trips are two weeks. Volunteers pay about $1,800, without

20   airfare. They usually stay in dormitories and cook their meals together. This year Earthwatch had 4,000 volunteers from 47 different countries.

     Cross-Cultural Solutions is another volunteer organization. It helps communities in China, Ghana, India, Peru, and Russia. Cross-Cultural Solutions helps to bring health care and education to many people. Twelve to eighteen vol-

25   unteers work together for about three weeks at one location. The work depends on the volunteers' skills. For instance, a volunteer may have special medical knowledge. This person will work in a local hospital. Volunteers have evenings and two weekends to spend on their own. Prices begin at $1,900 for a two-week trip, not including airfare.

People who take volunteer vacations believe they are helping people around the world to live healthier lives. They believe they can help people get an education. The people they help may have a better place to live. For the volunteers, this is the best vacation of all.

Read the passage once. Then read the following statements. Check whether they are True or False. If a statement is false, change the statement so that it is true. Then go back to the passage and find the line that supports your answer.

1. _____ True _____ False   Volunteer vacations are fun and relaxing.

_____

2. _____ True _____ False   Habitat for Humanity volunteers build houses all around the world.

_____

3. _____ True _____ False   Former U.S. President Jimmy Carter helps build houses for poor people.

_____

4. _____ True _____ False   Earthwatch helps doctors take care of people.

_____

5. _____ True _____ False   Cross-Cultural Solutions helps people with education.

_____

6. _____ True _____ False   All volunteer organizations pay the volunteers.

_____

7. _____ True _____ False   Volunteers pay for their own airfare.

_____

8. _____ True _____ False   Volunteer vacations are usually for only a week.

_____

Skimming and Scanning Exercise

PART 1

Skim through the passage. Then read the following statements. Choose the one that is the correct main idea of the reading.

a. Vacation volunteers receive money for helping people all around the world build their own homes.

b. Vacation volunteers work with organizations to help people around the world live better lives.

c. Vacation volunteers travel around the world to have fun and to relax in different countries.

PART 2

Work in small groups and complete the following chart about Volunteer Vacations.

	What do they do?	Where do they work?	How long is a volunteer vacation?	How much does it cost?
Habitat for Humanity				
Earthwatch				
Cross-Cultural Solutions				

Read each question carefully. Either circle the letter of the correct answer or write your answer in the space provided.

1. Volunteers are people who do something, but they receive no money for it. They do this because they want to be helpful to other people in need.

   a. **Volunteers** are people who
      1. work without pay
      2. need other people
      3. need some help

   b. **People in need**
      1. want someone to do something for them
      2. cannot always help themselves
      3. volunteer to help others

2. Volunteers need to be in good health. They build homes in the United States, but they also **construct** homes all over the world.

   Construct means
   a. volunteer
   b. condition
   c. build

3. Earthwatch gets many volunteers to help scientists do **research** in places around the world.

   Research means
   a. to study something carefully
   b. to do volunteer work
   c. to travel to different places

4. Earthwatch volunteers usually stay in **dormitories** and cook their meals together.

   Dormitories are

   a. individual homes

   b. group homes

   c. hotels

5. Twelve to eighteen volunteers work together for about three weeks at one **location.**

   A **location** is a

   a. job

   b. place

   c. person

6. Prices for Cross-Cultural Solutions **begin at** $1,900 for a two-week trip, not including airfare.

   a. **Begin at** $1,900 means

      1. $1,900 is the highest price

      2. $1,900 is the usual price

      3. $1,900 is the lowest price

   b. A two-week trip

      1. will cost at least $1,900. You also need to buy your own airplane ticket

      2. will usually cost $1,900. Your airplane ticket is part of the cost

      3. will always cost $1,900. You also need to buy your own airplane ticket

D. *Think* About It

Read the following questions and think about the answers. Write your answer below each question. Then, compare your answers with those of your classmates.

1. Former U.S. President Jimmy Carter is a volunteer for Habitat for Humanity. Why do you think Mr. Carter volunteers to help build houses for poor people?

   _____

   _____

2. Why do many people work so hard to help people they do not know, in countries they do not live in? What do you think?

   _____

   _____

E. DICTIONARY SKILLS

Read the dictionary entry for each word, and think about the context of the sentence. Write the number of the appropriate definition on the line next to the word. Then choose the sentence with the correct answer.

1.
> **former** *adj.* **1** previous, past; *He is a former employee of this company.* **2** referring to the first thing or person named in a pair; *n.* the first thing or person named in a pair: *We eat lots of fish and chicken, but we prefer the former* (meaning "the fish"). *See:* latter.

The most famous volunteer is **former** U.S. President Jimmy Carter.

a. **former:** _____

b. 1. The most famous volunteer is the past U.S. President Jimmy Carter.

    2. The most famous volunteer is the first in a pair of U.S. Presidents, Jimmy Carter.

2.
> **skill** *n.* **1** an ability to do s.t. well because of practice, talent, or special training: *She has excellent musical skills.* **2** a trade: *Plumbing is his skill.*

A volunteer for Cross-Cultural Solutions may have a **skill,** for example, special medical knowledge. This person will work in a local hospital.

a. **skill:** _____

b. 1. A volunteer may have the ability to do something well because of special training.

    2. A volunteer may have a trade.

In English, there are several ways that verbs change to nouns. Some verbs become nouns by adding the suffix *-tion,* for example, *collect (v.), collection (n.)*. In addition, some words change spelling, for example, *explain (v.), explanation (n.)*. Complete each sentence with the correct form of the words on the left. **Write all the verbs in the simple present tense. They may be affirmative or negative. The nouns may be singular or plural.**

solve *(v.)*
solution *(n.)*

1. a. Chris _____ his problems slowly. He thinks quickly.

    b. He thinks of several _____ right away, then chooses the best one.

educate *(v.)*
education *(n.)*

2. a. People around the world want all children to have a good _____.

    b. We usually _____ children in schools and at home.

locate *(v.)*
location *(n.)*

3. a. Volunteer organizations _____ communities in need.

    b. The _____ for volunteer work are usually in developing countries.

construct *(v.)*
construction *(n.)*

4. a. The _____ of a new home can be very fast when many volunteers work together.

    b. They _____ homes in many cities around the world.

organize *(v.)*
organization *(n.)*

5. a. When a volunteer _____ works well, it helps man people.

    b. Habitat for Humanity _____ groups of workers to build houses for people who cannot afford them.

Another Look

Read the following story about people who do volunteer work. Then answer the questions which follow.

Who Volunteers?

People volunteer in order to help other people in need. They also volunteer in order to "give back" to the community. This means that they want to help the people in their community who need help. However, volunteering is not only good for the community and those in need, but it is good for the volunteers, too. Volunteer Canada, an organization in Canada, started National Volunteer Week in 1943. Today, it is still very popular. In fact, six million people around the country volunteer.

Who volunteers? All kinds of people volunteer. For example, senior citizens (people over 65 years old) volunteer for many reasons. They want to meet new friends and stay active. Senior citizens often have a lot of free time. They can use this time to help other people. Sometimes, when people graduate from college, they do volunteer work. Then they can get some skills and experience before they find a job. Other people volunteer because it gives them a chance to do something different. New immigrants to Canada also volunteer. They get work experience and can improve their English and French language skills.

All of these volunteers in Canada do different work, but they have something in common: they are helping other people. And by helping other people, they are helping themselves, too.

QUESTIONS FOR ANOTHER LOOK

1. Who are **senior citizens?**
   a. Volunteers
   b. People over 65 years old
   c. College graduates

2. Who are **immigrants?**
   a. People who come from another country
   b. People who live in Canada
   c. People who volunteer

3. Who started National Volunteer Week in Canada?

   ____

4. Look at the chart below. Why do these people volunteer? Write the reasons.

Volunteers	Why do they volunteer?
1. Senior citizens	
2. College graduates	
3. New immigrants	

What can volunteers do for people in need? Make a list.

...jine you are going to interview the director of National ...ake a list of questions you want to ask this person. ...of questions with those of your classmates.

I.   Topics FOR *Discussion* AND *Writing*

1. This chapter discusses three volunteer organizations. Which one do you think does the most important work? Why? Write your reasons and give examples.

2. Former U.S. President Jimmy Carter is very famous. Do you think it is a good idea for famous people to volunteer to help others? Why? Explain your reasons.

3. What was your favorite vacation? Why? Who did you go with? Write about what you did on your favorite vacation.

4. **Write in your journal.** Will you ever volunteer to work with an organization such as Habitat for Humanity, Earthwatch, or Cross-Cultural Solutions? If so, which one? Why? If not, why not?

Word Search

Read the words listed below. Find them in the puzzle and circle them. They may be written in any direction.

airfare	famous	location	vacation
construct	healthy	organizations	volunteer
dormitories	helpful	research	world

```
S  H  E  L  P  F  U  L  R  V  G  R  J  C  T
R  E  M  Q  T  H  X  S  A  U  Y  S  I  M  C
E  N  I  R  E  T  H  C  R  H  U  C  S  K  U
S  M  W  R  E  H  A  E  T  G  K  E  Q  Q  R
E  L  V  W  O  T  E  L  U  J  B  B  U  N  T
A  S  N  O  I  T  A  Z  I  N  A  G  R  O  S
R  V  C  O  N  E  I  L  O  C  A  T  I  O  N
C  R  N  U  H  B  D  M  T  R  R  P  P  F  O
H  X  L  M  N  B  R  L  R  N  U  I  R  G  C
H  O  S  U  O  M  A  F  R  O  W  K  H  Y  Z
V  A  U  R  H  V  R  H  T  O  D  T  X  O  H
E  R  A  F  R  I  A  I  X  V  W  F  P  H  Q
```

Crossword Puzzle

Read the clues on the next page. Write the answers in the correct spaces in the puzzle.

Crossword Puzzle Clues

Across Clues

1. Build
5. Time off from work
8. Study something carefully
9. Previous; past
10. Answer to a problem
11. Earthwatch, Habitat for Humanity, Cross-Cultural Solutions are all _____
13. We go to school to get an _____.
14. People who work without being paid

Down Clues

2. Abilities
3. Peru, Russia, Honduras, China are all _____.
4. An endangered animal in Florida
6. Place
7. Group home
12. The price of an airplane ticket

UNIT 1 DISCUSSION

1. The idea of a family traveling throughout the country is a common American vacation. How is this way of traveling all-American? How does a trip like this characterize American culture?

2. Many people around the world volunteer during their vacation to help other people. What other ways can people volunteer to help others?

Grammar Cloze Quiz

Read the passage below. Complete each blank space with an article: from the box

a	an	the

Everyone enjoys taking _____ vacation. _____
(1)   (2)
vacation is fun and relaxing. Some people like to go to _____
(3)
beach and swim. Other people go to the mountains, or visit

_____ unusual country. Many other people take
(4)

_____ volunteer vacation to help other people. Volunteers are
(5)

people who do something because they want to be helpful to other people

in need. Many organizations give volunteers _____ chance to
(6)

help others.

Habitat for Humanity is _____ organization of volunteers
(7)

who build homes for _____ poor. _____ most
(8)   (9)

famous volunteer is former U.S. President Jimmy Carter, who won

_____ Nobel Prize for Peace. Habitat for Humanity volunteers
(10)

don't need _____ special skills. They just need to be in good
(11)

health. Volunteers build homes in _____ United States, but they
(12)

also construct homes all over _____ world.
(13)

_____ second organization is called Earthwatch. Earthwatch
(14)

volunteers may study _____ endangered animal such as mana-
(15)

tees in Florida.

1. A "Habitat for Humanity" project in Durban, South Africa, will be described in the video. What do you remember about Habitat for Humanity? Why do you think these people are volunteering in South Africa?

2. Read the facts and numbers below. Then watch and listen to the video once or twice. Match the facts in the column on the left with the numbers in the column on the right. Put the correct letter on the line after each fact.

   1. Number of people living in shacks in South Africa _____
   2. Number of years the Carters have helped construct houses _____
   3. Patience Lisa's pay in dollars per month _____
   4. Number of houses built in South Africa since 1994 _____
   5. Number of former presidents working on the project shown in the video _____

   a. two
   b. over a million
   c. more than 7 million
   d. 19
   e. less than 100

3. According to the mayor of Durban, the Habitat for Humanity project resembles "an old African tradition." What is that tradition? Why is that tradition important?

Surfing THE INTERNET

Do you or does someone you know volunteer? Search the Internet for volunteer opportunities in your city. Go to a search engine such as Google, MSN, or Yahoo and enter the word **volunteer** and the name of your city. Look over the volunteer jobs available and tell your class about them.

Optional Activity: Visit the Habitat for Humanity website at www.habitat.org and read about the organization. Then click on "Where We Build" (www.habitat.org/local/). Are there Habitat projects helping people in need in your country or community? Find the nearest projects and tell your class about them.

UNIT 2

FAMILY LIFE

3

How Alike Are Identical Twins?

Prereading Preparation

1. Look at the photograph. Describe the two people.

2. Read the title of this passage. What will the reading tell you about?

3. Choose the sentences which describe identical twins.

_____ a. They are always both boys or both girls.

_____ b. Identical twins can be a boy and a girl.

_____ c. Identical twins always have the same color hair.

_____ d. One identical twin can have dark hair and the other can have light hair.

_____ e. Identical twins always have the same color eyes.

_____ f. One identical twin may have blue eyes, and the other may have brown eyes.

_____ g. As adults, identical twins will be the same height.

_____ h. As adults, one identical twin may be taller than the other.

How Alike Are Identical Twins?

Most twins who grew up together are very close. John and Buell Fuller are 79-year-old identical twins. They have always lived together, and still do. They wear identical clothes and work together, too. They think it is funny that people can't tell them apart. In fact, they like to confuse people. Sometimes John tells people he is Buell, and sometimes Buell tells people he is John.

Identical twins like the Fullers are very unusual in the United States. Out of every 1,000 births, there are only four pairs of identical twins. Naturally, most people are very curious about them. Scientists want to know about twins, too. Do twins feel the same pain? Do they think the same thoughts? Do they share these thoughts?

Scientists understand how twins are born. Now, though, they are trying to explain how being half of a biological pair influences a twin's identity. They want to know why many identical twins make similar choices even when they don't live near each other. For example, Jim Springer and Jim Lewis are identical twins. They were separated when they were only four months old.

The two Jims grew up in different families and did not meet for 39 years. When they finally met, they discovered some surprising similarities between them. Both men were married twice. Their first wives were named Linda and their second wives were both named Betty! Both twins named their first sons James Allan, drove blue Chevrolets, and had dogs named Toy. Are all these facts coincidences, or are they biological?

Scientists want to know what influences our personality. They study pairs of identical twins who grew up in different surroundings, like Jim Springer and Jim Lewis. These twins help scientists understand the connection between environment and biology. Researchers at the University of Minnesota studied 350 sets of identical twins who did not grow up together. They discovered many similarities in their personalities. Scientists believe that personality characteristics such as friendliness, shyness, and fears are not a result of environment. These characteristics are probably inherited.

Some pairs of identical twins say that they have ESP[1] experiences. For instance, some twins say that they can feel when their twin is in pain or in trouble. Twins also seem to be closer and more open to each other's thoughts and feelings than other brothers and sisters. For example, Donald and Louis Keith are close in this way. The Keiths are identical twins. Donald says that by concentrating very hard, he can make Louis telephone him.

Scientists continue to study identical twins because they are uncertain about them and have many questions. For example, they are still unsure about the connection between environment and personality. They want to know: can twins really communicate without speaking? Can one twin really feel another twin's pain? Perhaps with more research, scientists will find the answers.

1. ESP: Extrasensory Perception. ESP is the ability to feel something that people cannot feel with the five senses.

A.　Fact-Finding Exercise

Read the passage once. Then read the following statements. Check whether they are True or False. If a statement is false, rewrite the statement so that it is true. Then go back to the passage and find the line that supports your answer.

1. ____ True ____ False   Scientists want to know about identical twins.

_____

2. ____ True ____ False   Jim Springer and Jim Lewis always lived together.

_____

3. ____ True ____ False   Scientists understand twins better when they study twins who grew up together.

_____

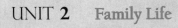

4. _____ True _____ False   John and Buell Fuller were separated at birth and did not grow up together.

_____

5. ✓ True _____ False   Some identical twins have ESP experiences about each other.

_____

6. ✓ True _____ False   Scientists believe that people are born with friendly, shy, or fearful personalities.

_____

Skimming and Scanning Exercise

PART 1

Skim through the passage. Then read the following statements. Choose the one that is the correct main idea of the reading.

a. John and Buell Fuller, typical identical twins, grew up together.

b. Identical twins are very unusual in the United States.

c. Doctors believe that identical twins are very similar in both their looks and their personalities.

PART 2

Scan the passage. Work with a partner to fill in the chart below with information from the reading.

IDENTICAL TWINS

	Their Names	Similarities between Them
Twins Who Grew Up Together		
Twins Who Grew Up Apart		
University of Minnesota Study a. Which identical twins did the researchers study? b. How many sets of twins did researchers study? c. Why did researchers study them?	a. b. c.	
What characteristics of twins may be inherited?		

Reading Analysis

Read each question carefully. Either circle the letter of the correct answer, or write your answer in the space provided.

1. Most twins who grew up together are very **close.** John and Buell Fuller are 79-year-old identical twins. They have always lived together, and **still do.** They wear identical clothes and work together, too. They think it is amusing that people **can't tell them apart.**

   a. In this paragaraph, **close** means that they
      1. live near each other
      2. live in the same house
      3. are very good friends

   b. What do John and Buell Fuller **still do?**
      1. Confuse people
      2. Live together
      3. Wear the same clothes

   c. People **can't tell them apart.** This means that they
      1. look exactly the same
      2. people can't talk to them alone
      3. they never work apart

2. Out of every 1,000 births, there are only four pairs of identical twins. This sentence means that
   a. if 1,000 women have babies, four women will have identical twins.
   b. only four pairs of identical twins are born in the U.S. every year.

3. Most people **are very curious** about identical twins. Scientists want to know about twins, too. Do twins feel the same pain? Do they think the same thoughts? Do they share these thoughts?

   In these sentences, which word or phrase is a synonym for **are very curious?**
   a. Feel
   b. Want to know
   c. Think

4. Scientists understand how twins are born. Now, though, they are trying to explain how **being half of a biological pair** influences a twin's identity.

   Being half of a biological pair means being

   a. a scientist

   b. a twin

   c. alone

5. Jim Springer and Jim Lewis are famous identical twins. They were separated when they were only four months old. **The two Jims** grew up in different families and did not meet for 39 years. **Both** men were married twice. Their first wives were named Linda and their second wives were **both** named Betty!

   a. Who are the **two Jims?**

   _____

   b. How many is **both?**

      1. Two

      2. Four

      3. Six

6. Both Jim Springer and Jim Lewis named their first sons James Allen. Both Jims drove blue Chevrolets. They both had dogs named Toy. Are all these facts simply **coincidences?**

   a. A **coincidence** is something that happens

      1. by plan, or arrangement

      2. by accident, or chance

   b. Read the following sentences. Decide which situation is a coincidence.

      1. Dean telephoned Jenny and invited her to have lunch with him. They decided to meet at 1 o'clock in front of The Palace Restaurant. Jenny arrived at 1 o'clock, and Dean arrived at 1:05. They said "Hi" to each other, and went into the restaurant.

      2. Dean and Jenny sat at a table in the restaurant. Jenny saw her sister, Christine, at the next table! Jenny and Christine greeted each other, and they all had lunch together at the same table.

7. Scientists want to know what influences our personality. **Pairs** of identical twins who grew up in different **surroundings,** like Jim Springer and Jim Lewis, help scientists understand the connection between environment and biology. Researchers at the University of Minnesota studied 350 sets of identical twins who did not grow up together.

   a. In this paragraph, which word is a synonym of **pairs?**

   _____

   b. In this paragraph, which word is a synonym of **surroundings?**

   _____

   c. What do the two words in "b" mean?
      1. The house you live in
      2. The place you live in
      3. The people you live with
      4. All of the above

8. Scientists believe that personality characteristics such as friendliness, shyness, and fears are not a result of environment. **They** are inherited.

   a. What are some examples of personality characteristics?

   _____

   b. How do you know?

   _____

   c. What does **they** refer to?
      1. Scientists
      2. Personality characteristics
      3. Fears

9. Other pairs of identical twins say that they have **ESP** experiences.

   a. Look at page 39. What is **ESP?**

   _____

   b. How do you know?

   _____

   c. This type of information is called a
      1. preface.
      2. footnote.
      3. direction.

10. Donald and Louis Keith are very close. **The Keiths** are identical twins. Donald says that **by concentrating very hard, he can make Louis telephone him.**

    a. Who are **the Keiths?**

    _____

    b. What does Donald mean?

       1. Donald tells Louis to call him, and Louis calls him.

       ②. Donald thinks about Louis, and Louis calls him.

11. Scientists continue to study identical twins because they are **uncertain** about them and have many questions. However, most twins are sure about one fact: being a twin is wonderful because you are never alone and you always have a best friend!

    In this paragraph, what word means the opposite of **uncertain?**

    _____

D. *Think* About It

Read the following questions and think about the answers. Write your answers below each question. Then, compare your answers with those of your classmates.

1. Scientists want to study identical twins who did not grow up together. They want to understand the connection between environment and biology. Why are these identical twins so helpful to scientists?

    _____

    _____

    _____

2. Scientists believe that friendliness, shyness, and fears are inherited. What personality characteristics do you think are the result of environment?

    _____

    _____

    _____

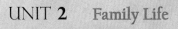

E. DICTIONARY SKILLS

Read the dictionary entry for each word, and think about the context of the sentence. Write the number of the appropriate definition on the line next to the word. Then choose the sentence with the correct answer.

1.

> **concentrate** *v.* **-trated, -trating, -trates**
> **1** to think hard about s.t., *(syn.)* to focus one's attention: *During exams, students concentrate hard on answering the questions.*
> **2** to reduce the amount of s.t. and increase its strength, *(syn.)* to **condense:** *Orange juice that is concentrated can be stored in the freezer. -n.* [C;U] a condensed form of s.t.: *a chemical concentrate*

Donald and Louis Keith are identical twins. Donald says that by **concentrating** very hard, he can make Louis telephone him.

a. **concentrate:** _____

b. 1. Donald says that by increasing his strength, he can make Louis telephone him.

2. Donald says that by focusing his attention on Louis, he can make Louis telephone him.

3. Donald says that by reducing the amount of his strength, he can make Louis telephone him.

2.

> **close** (1) *adj.* **closer, closest 1** with little space between, nearby: *Her chair is close to the wall.* **2** near in time: *It's close to 5:00.* **3** very friendly, *(syn.)* **intimate:** *They are a close family with a few close friends.* **4** with air that is not fresh and is usu. too warm, *(syn.)* **stuffy:** *It is very close in this room; let's open a window.*
>
> **5** with strict control: *The doctor put her patient under close observation.* **6** a close call: s.t. that is difficult to judge: *The two runners crossed the finish line together, so who won was a close call* (or) *too close to call.* a narrow escape from danger or death: *The speeding taxi nearly hit him; that was a close call.* (or) *a close shave. -adv.* **closely;** *-n.* **closeness.**

Twins also seem to be closer and more open to each other's thoughts and feelings than other brothers and sisters. For example, Donald and Louis Keith are identical twins, and they are close in this way.

a. **close:** _____

b. 1. Donald and Louis are intimate in this way.

2. Donald and Louis are nearby in this way.

3. Donald and Louis are stuffy in this way.

3.

> **environment** *n.* **1** [C;U] the air, land,
> water, and surroundings that people, plants,
> and animals live in: *The environment in big
> cities is usually polluted.* **2** [C] a set of
> social conditions that affect people, an
> atmosphere: *That child is growing up in a
> bad environment. -adj.* **environmental**; *-adv.*
> **environmentally.**

Scientists study pairs of identical twins who grew up in different surroundings, like Jim Springer and Jim Lewis. These twins help scientists understand the connection between biology and environment.

a. **environment:** _____

b. 1. Identical twins who did not grow up together help scientists understand the connection between biology and the air, land, water, and surroundings that twins live in.

   2. Identical twins who did not grow up together help scientists understand the connection between biology and the social conditions that affect people.

PART 1

In English, some adjectives become nouns by adding the suffix -*ness,* for example, *loud (adj.), loudness (n.).* Read each sentence. Write the correct form of the word on the left. Be careful of spelling changes, for example, *dry (adj.), dryness (n.)* but *happy (adj.), happiness (n.).* Complete each sentence with the correct form of the words on the left. **The nouns are all singular.**

close *(adj.)*
closeness *(n.)*

1.   a.   Winnie and Loretta are good friends. They are very
         _____ and tell each other everything.
   b.   Their _____ will continue for many years.

sure *(adj.)*
sureness *(n.)*

2.   a.   Jonathan is absolutely _____ that the movie
         begins at 9:30.
   b.   Because of his _____ , we left for the movie
         theater at 8:30.

open *(adj.)*
openness *(n.)*

3.   a.   Jimmy has a special _____ that many people like.
   b.   He makes friends easily with his warm, _____
         personality.

friendly *(adj.)*
friendliness *(n.)*

4.   a.   All the people at Jodi's party are very _____
         to me.
   b.   Their _____ makes me feel comfortable, and I'm
         having a good time.

shy *(adj.)*
shyness *(n.)*

5.   a.   Unfortunately, Raymond's _____ stops him from
         making friends.
   b.   He is too _____ to talk to people he doesn't
         know.

In English, the noun form and the verb form of some words are the same, for example, *cover (v.), cover (n.)*. Read each sentence. Write the correct form of the word on the left. Then circle (*v.*) if you are using a verb or (*n.*) if you are using a noun. **Write all the verbs in the simple present tense. The verbs may be negative or positive. The nouns may be singular or plural.**

influence

1. a. Our parents often have a strong _____ on our lives. *(v., n.)*

    b. They usually _____ us in positive ways.
        (v., n.)

fear

2. a. Tom has very few _____.
        (v., n.)

    b. However, when Tom goes to bed, he always _____ that he will die in his sleep. *(v., n.)*

experience

3. a. Sometimes a twin _____ an ESP event.
        (v., n.)

    b. When he does, he usually calls his twin to see if his twin had the same _____.
        (v., n.)

work

4. a. Lisa _____ at night. She only works during the day.
        (v., n.)

    b. Her _____ is very interesting. She writes
        (v., n.)
        educational computer programs.

telephone

5. a. Please answer the _____. It is ringing.
        (v., n.)

    b. I think it is my brother. He _____ me every day at this time. *(v., n.)*

Read the description of a father's diary about the birth of his triplets and their life experiences. Then answer the questions which follow.

Diary of a Triplet Father

Birth to six months: When the doctor told us that we were pregnant with triplets, we were surprised, and wondered what the future would be. We quickly found out after we brought our three babies home.

The first six months of parenthood is a difficult learning experience. We wrote everything down, especially feeding times and how much food the babies ate. We even had to chart diaper changes (960 the first month!). We marked all the toys, bottles, and clothes with a different color for each child so they could sense what is theirs.

Six months to four years: It was hardest for us to get used to all the equipment. We had three of everything: car seats, portable cribs, high chairs, diaper bags, and changes of clothes, not to mention toys!

At this time of life, every minute is a new discovery. Even though you try very hard, you will never be able to carefully watch all three of them at once! Every two-year-old must touch and taste everything, but everything must also be shared by the triplets. We soon learned that they each wanted whatever their sibling had at that moment.

When they began to speak, my wife noticed that they had their own names for each other. When we began to make note of the particular sounds that they said to each other, we realized that they had their own language. The age that we have the happiest memories of is two.

School age: When it was time to send the children to school, they went to three different classes. Kindergarten and first grade were easier for the kids than they were for us. They each had plenty of arts and crafts homework. Since they had three different assignments, homework lasted a long time. Second grade seems to be less of a problem at homework time because they are able to do more work without our help.

The triplets don't always get along. Sometimes they fight just like other brothers and sisters. However, there is still a bond between them that my wife and I hope never disappears.

QUESTIONS FOR ANOTHER LOOK

Read the following list of **Life Experiences.** Put them in the correct category on the next page.

1. Homework lasted a long time because they had different assignments.

2. The triplets had their own language.

3. The parents wrote down feeding times and how much food each baby ate.

4. It was hard for the parent to get used to all the equipment.

5. The parents wrote down diaper changes.

6. Homework time became easier in second grade because the triplets needed less help.

7. The triplets touch and taste everything.

8. The triplets had their own names for each other.

9. The parents marked all toys, clothes, and bottles with a different color.

10. Each triplet wants what the other one has.

11. The triplets each went to different kindergarten classes.

Birth to Six Months	Six Months to Four Years	School Age
_____	_____	_____
_____	_____	_____
_____	_____	_____
_____	_____	_____

1. Work in pairs. Imagine you are going to interview a set of identical twins. These twins did not grow up together. In fact, they did not meet until they were 30 years old. Make up a list of questions to ask the twins. You want to find out how they are similar. Compare your list of questions with those of your classmates.

2. Work in pairs. Imagine you are going to interview a set of identical twins. These twins *did* grow up together. Make up a list of questions to ask the twins. You want to find out how they are similar. Compare your list of questions with those of your classmates.

3. If you can find a set of twins or triplets, interview them. Use the questions you have prepared. Report back to the class.

I. Topics FOR Discussion AND Writing

1. Do you know any twins or triplets? Write about them. Tell who they are. Describe how they are alike, and how they are different.

2. Explain why you think being a twin may be a positive or a negative experience. Explain your positive reasons and your negative reasons.

3. **Write in your journal.** Imagine that you have a twin brother or sister. What do you like best about having a twin? What do you like least about having a twin?

Word Search

Read the words listed below. Find them in the puzzle and circle them. They may be written in any direction.

alike	confuse	identical	personality
biological	different	influence	separate
concentrate	environment	inherited	twins

E	N	V	I	R	O	N	M	E	N	T	Y	E	I	O
L	E	K	I	L	A	U	C	B	N	T	T	R	N	A
R	A	O	T	W	I	N	S	E	I	A	H	L	H	N
L	F	C	Z	K	E	W	R	L	R	L	A	R	E	K
U	R	Q	I	U	R	E	A	T	H	C	Q	T	R	M
V	Q	Z	L	G	F	N	N	A	I	C	A	B	I	X
X	N	F	G	F	O	E	J	T	A	R	R	C	T	H
J	N	E	I	S	C	L	N	Z	A	V	O	Y	E	W
I	E	D	R	N	G	E	O	P	Q	N	B	F	D	H
T	Y	E	O	N	D	I	E	I	F	Y	J	J	N	M
W	P	C	K	I	E	S	G	U	B	A	Y	H	A	I
L	Y	T	J	Z	Y	C	S	J	G	N	T	M	C	D
E	D	F	W	R	S	E	B	R	T	O	J	N	Q	W

Read the clues on the next page. Write the answers in the correct spaces in the puzzle.

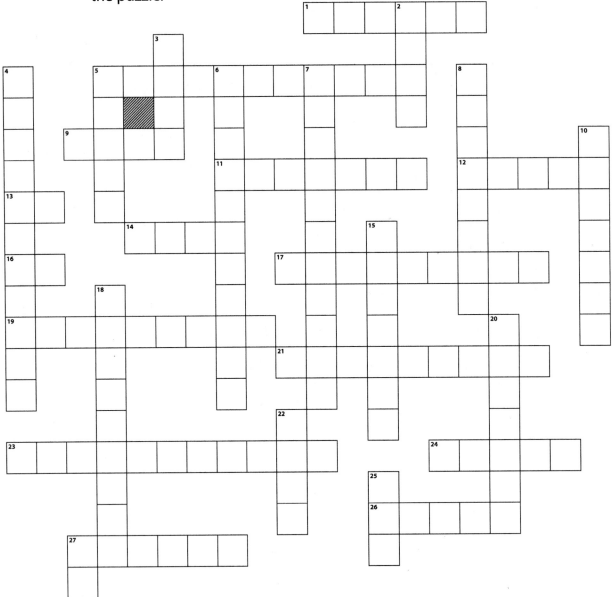

Crossword Puzzle Clues

Across Clues

1. The opposite of **after**

5. A _____ is something that happens accidentally, without planning.

9. Saturday and Sunday are _____ days of the week.

11. Cats are very _____ animals. They want to know about everything.

12. Do you sit _____ all your classmates, or do you sit alone?

13. The opposite of **off**

14. The opposite of **up**

16. I will meet you _____ 6 o'clock.

17. The color of your hair and your eyes are _____ from your parents.

19. _____ means **exactly the same.**

21. Not sure

23. A _____ is a person who studies something very carefully.

24. The opposite of **above**

26. People cannot live _____ water.

27. The opposite of **in front of**

Down Clues

2. The opposite of **under**

3. I don't want to go to the movies alone. I want to go _____ you.

4. Your _____ is your character, your way of behaving.

5. Kathy and Laura are very good friends. They are very _____.

6. When I think very hard about something, I _____ on it.

7. Our surroundings are our _____.

8. Not together; apart

10. She does not like that idea. She is _____ it. She is not in favor of it.

15. The United States is _____ Canada and Mexico.

18. Our family, our education, and our home all have an _____ on us. They all affect us.

20. Almost alike; very close in appearance

22. I received a letter _____ my friend yesterday. Tomorrow I will write a letter to her.

25. The opposite of **in**

27. We come to class _____ bus.

they

'hem

their

ınk space with one of the
onouns more than once.

e born. Now, though,

ın how being half of a biological pair

in___.   _____ want to know why many
                                           (3)

identical twins ι.   .s even when _____ don't live
                                                      (4)

near each other. For exampιc,   Springer and Jim Lewis are identical twins.

Jim Springer was separated from Jim Lewis when _____ were
                                                         (5)

only four months old. Jim Springer did not meet _____ brother
                                                            (6)

Jim Lewis for 39 years. When Jim Springer finally met _____,
                                                                 (7)

_____ discovered some similarities between _____.
         (8)   (9)

Both men were married twice. _____ first wives were named
                                        (10)

Linda and _____ second wives were both named Betty! Both
                  (11)

twins named _____ first sons James Allan, drove blue
                      (12)

Chevrolets, and had dogs named Toy. Are all these facts coincidences, or are

_____ biological? How can we explain _____?
         (13)   (14)

4

The Search for Happiness through Adoption

Prereading Preparation

1. Look at the photograph. Describe the man and the woman. Describe the child. Do you think this child is this man and woman's biological child? Explain your reason.

2. **Adoption** means that
   a. people have children of their own
   b. people take another person's child as their own

3. What kinds of children do people adopt? For example, small babies, older children, boys, girls, children from different countries.

4. Read the title. Who is searching for happiness?
   a. People who adopt children
   b. Children who are adopted
   c. The people who adopt children and the children they adopt

5. Work with one or two partners. Why do people adopt children? Why do people give up a child for adoption? Make a list of reasons. When you finish, compare your list with those of your classmates.

Reasons people adopt a child:	Reasons people give up a child for adoption:

The Search for Happiness through Adoption

1   When couples get married, they usually plan to have children. Sometimes, however, a couple cannot have a child of their own. In this case, they may decide to adopt a child. In fact, adoption is very common today. There are about 130,000 adoptions each year in the United States alone. Some people prefer to adopt
5   infants; others adopt older children. Some couples adopt children from their own countries; others adopt children from foreign countries. Some people adopt children of their same race, i.e., white, black, Asian; others adopt children of different races. In any case, they all adopt children for the same reason: they care about children, and want to give their adopted child a happy life. This includes a
10 comfortable home, a loving family, and a good education.

    Most adopted children know that they are adopted. Psychologists and child care experts generally think this is a good idea. However, many adopted children, or adoptees, have very little information about their biological mother and father. As a matter of fact, it is often very difficult for adoptees to find out about their
15 birth parents because the birth records of most adoptees are usually sealed. The information is confidential, so no one can see it. Sealed documents protect both adoptees and their natural parents.

    Naturally, adopted children have different feelings about their birth parents. Many adoptees want to search for them, but others do not. Jake, who is thirteen,
20 was adopted when he was only two and a half months old. He says, "I don't think I'll ever search out my birth mother. I might want to get some more facts, but I don't feel I really want to go looking. Maybe she would be awful and I'd just be

disappointed." Carla, who is twelve, was adopted when she was four years old. Her adoptive parents also adopted another little girl. Carla says, "Sometimes my sister and I will talk. She says she doesn't want to look for her birth mother when she gets older, but I have mixed feelings. Sometimes I feel that I want to look for her—and my mother says she'll help me when I'm older—but sometimes I don't want to look for her at all because I'm scared of finding out what her reactions would be. I worry that she'll have a whole new life and I'll just be interfering with that new life. She might not want anyone to know about her past." Sue, who is thirteen, was adopted when she was a baby. Her family helped her find her birth mother. Sue says, "I think adopted kids should be allowed to search whenever they're ready. They need to know where they came from. And they need to know what their medical history is. As soon as I searched and found the information I was looking for, I felt more worthwhile in the world. Beforehand, a part of me had always been missing."

The decision to search for birth parents is a difficult one to make. Most adoptees, like Carla, have mixed feelings about finding their biological parents. Even though adoptees do not know about their past or their natural parents, they *do* know that their adoptive parents want them, love them, and will care for them.

Fact-Finding Exercise

Read the passage once. Then read the following statements. Check whether they are True or False. If the statement is false, rewrite the statement so that it is true. Then go back to the passage and find the line that supports your answer.

1. _____ True _____ False   Adoption is common in the United States.

   _____

2. _____ True _____ False   People only adopt babies of their same race.

   _____

3. _____ True _____ False   Most adopted children don't know they are adopted.

   _____

4. _____ True _____ False   It is easy for adopted children to find their birth parents.

   _____

5. _____ True _____ False   Most adoption birth records are confidential.

   _____

6. _____ True _____ False   Jake wants to find his birth mother.

   _____

7. _____ True _____ False   Sue found her birth mother.

   _____

PART 1

Skim through the passage. Then read the following statements. Choose the one that is the correct main idea of the reading.

    a.   Most adopted children know they are adopted, but not all of them want to find their natural parents.

    b.   Some couples adopt children when they cannot have children of their own.

    c.   People adopt children of different ages, races, and from different countries.

PART 2

Scan the passage. Work with a partner to fill in the chart below with information from the reading.

Feelings About Adoption		
Name	**Do These People Think It Is A Good Idea To Find Birth Parents?**	**Reasons**
Childcare Experts	Yes/No/I don't know	
Jake	Yes/No/I don't know	
Carla	Yes/No/I don't know	
Sue	Yes/No/I don't know	

Read each question carefully. Circle the letter or the number of the correct answer, or write your answer on the blank line.

!, they usually plan to have children. Sometimes,
have a child of their own. **In this case,** they may
fact, adoption is very common today. There are
; in the United States alone.

;not have children
ns to have children
:s married

option
about adoption
option

c. The last sentence means that

   1. the United States is the only country in the world where people adopt children

   2. about 130,000 adoptions take place in the United States, and many adoptions take place in other countries, too

   3. people who adopt children in the United States are alone

d. What does **about 130,000** mean?

   1. More than 130,000

   2. Less than 130,000

   3. Around 130,000

2. Some people prefer to adopt **infants;** others adopt older children. What is an **infant?**

   a. A very young baby

   b. A small child

   c. A young child

3. Some people adopt children of their same race, **e.g.,** white, black, Asian; others adopt children of different races. **In any case,** they all adopt children for the same reason: they care about children, and want to give their adopted child a happy life. **This** includes a comfortable home, a loving family, a good education.

   a. What does **e.g.** mean?
       1. For example
       2. The same race
       3. Also

   b. What does **in any case** mean?
       1. When people adopt children of the same race
       2. It does not matter what kind of child they adopt.
       3. If they adopt a child of a different race

   c. What information follows the colon (:)?
       1. An example
       2. An opposite idea
       3. A reason

   d. What does **this** refer to?
       1. A good education
       2. A happy life
       3. A loving family

4. Most adopted children know that they are adopted. Psychologists and child care experts generally think **this** is a good idea.

   This refers to the fact that
   a. children know they are adopted
   b. people want to adopt children

5. Many adopted children, or **adoptees,** have very little information about their **biological mother and father. As a matter of fact,** it is often very difficult for adoptees to find out about their birth parents because the birth **records** of most adoptees are usually **sealed.** The information is **confidential,** so no one can see it. Sealed documents protect both adoptees and their natural parents.

    a. What does **adoptees** mean?
        1. Children who are adopted
        2. People who adopt children

    b. In this paragraph, what are synonyms for the words **biological mother and father?**

        _____

    c. What information follows **as a matter of fact?**
        1. More information about the same idea
        2. Different information about the previous idea

    d. Read the following sentence, and complete it.
        The weather today is very cold. As a matter of fact,
        1. tomorrow will be cold, too
        2. the temperature is below freezing

    e. Which word in this paragraph is a synonym for **records?**

        _____

    f. What are **sealed** documents?
        1. They are documents that are in an envelope.
        2. They are documents that no one can read.

    g. What does **confidential** mean?
        1. Important
        2. Serious
        3. Secret

6. **Naturally,** adopted children have different feelings about their birth parents. Many adoptees want to **search for** them, but others **do not.**

    a. **Naturally** means
        1. of course
        2. however

b. What does **do not** mean?

    1. Other adoptees do not want to search for their birth parents.

    2. Other adoptees do not have different feelings about their birth parents.

7. Carla says, "My sister says she doesn't want to look for her birth mother, but I have **mixed feelings.** Sometimes I feel that I want to look for her—and my mother says she'll help me when I'm older—but sometimes I don't want to look for her because I'm scared of finding out what her reactions would be."

    a. Why does Carla says that she has **mixed feelings?**

        1. She does not want to look for her natural mother.

        2. She wants to look for her natural mother.

        3. She is not sure what she wants to do.

    b. When you have **mixed feelings,** you

        1. think two opposite ways about something

        2. think differently from another person

8. Sue says, "Adopted kids need to know where they came from, and they need to know what their medical history is. As soon as I searched and found the information I was looking for, I felt more **worthwhile** in the world. **Beforehand,** a part of me had always been missing."

    a. **Worthwhile** means

        1. unsure

        2. happy

        3. important

    b. **Beforehand** refers to the time

        1. before something happens

        2. after something happens

    c. Jack was on time when he arrived at the station to take the train. Beforehand,

        1. he went to bed early last night

        2. he had called the station to find out the train schedule

9. **Even though** adoptees do not know about their past or their natural parents, they **do** know that their adoptive parents want them, love them, and will care for them.

  a. What does **even though** mean?
    1. Also
    2. Although
    3. However

  b. Complete the following sentence.
    Even though the train was late,
    1. Karen arrived at work on time
    2. Karen was late to work

  c. Why is **do** before the verb, and why is it in italics?
    1. To show emphasis
    2. To ask a question

D. *Think* About It

Read the following questions and think about the answers. Write your answers below the questions. Then, compare your answers with those of your classmates.

1. What might be some reasons why some people adopt children from foreign countries?

  _____

  _____

  _____

2. What might be some reasons why adoptees want or need to find information about their natural parents?

  _____

  _____

  _____

E. DICTIONARY SKILLS

Read the dictionary entry for each word, and think about the context of the sentence. Write the number of the appropriate definition on the line next to the word. Then choose the sentence with the correct answer.

1.

> **care** *v.* **cared, caring, cares 1** to feel concern about the well-being of others: *She cares about everyone; she is interested in and concerned about people.* || *He doesn't care about anyone but himself.* **2** to be concerned about s.t., *(syn.)* to **worry:** *She cares about the quality of her work.* || *I really want to buy that car; I don't care if it costs too much!* **3** not to care for: to like or love: *(love) I don't care for her.* || *(like) He doesn't care for carrots or beans.* **4** *phrasal v. insep.* **to care for s.o. or s.t.:** to look after s.o.'s health, *(syn.)* to **nurse:** *When she was sick, he cared for her day and night.* **5 to not care less:** to not care at all: *He is such a bad manager; I could not care less if he leaves the company.*

People adopt children because they **care** about them, and want to give their adopted child a happy life.

a. **care:** _____

b. 1. People adopt children because they worry about them.

2. People adopt children because they are concerned about the children's well-being.

3. People adopt children because they want to look after their health.

2.

> **record** *n.* **1** s.t. (usu. written) that proves that an event happened, including records of business transactions, scientific data, cultural, or other human activities: *The records of our business are kept in our computer and in printouts.* **2** the best time, distance, etc., in an athletic event: *She holds the world record for the 100-meter dash.* **3** a criminal's history of arrests and things he or she did wrong: *That thief has a long criminal record.* **4** a flat, black disk onto which a sound recording, esp. music, has been pressed: *He has a collection of Elvis Presley records from the 1950s.*

The birth **records** of most adoptees are usually sealed because the information is confidential.

a. **record:** _____

b. 1. Written information about an adoptee's birth is confidential.

   2. The criminal history of an adoptee's birth is confidential.

   3. Information about an adoptee's birth is written on a flat, black disk.

3.

> **history** *n.,*-**ies** **1** [C; U] the study of past events (people, civilizations, etc.): *She studied European history at college.* **2** [C] past events, or a written account of past events: *My family history is very interesting; I plan to write it all down some day.* ‖ *She read a history of Peru.* **3** **that's history or past (ancient) history:** s.t. that is no longer important: *His bad behavior is past history; he's a good boy now.* **4** **to make history:** to do s.t. memorable, important.

Sue says, "Adopted kids need to know where they came from, and they need to know what their medical **history** is."

a. **history:** _____

b. 1. Adopted children need to find written accounts of their medical records.

   2. Adopted children need to study their past.

   3. Adopted children make their own history.

PART 1

In English, there are several ways that verbs change to nouns. Some verbs become nouns by adding the suffix, -ion, for example, *suggest (v.), suggestion (n.)*. Complete each sentence with the correct form of the words on the left. **Write all the verbs in the simple present tense. They may be affirmative or negative. The nouns may be singular or plural.**

decide *(v.)*
decision *(n.)*

1. a. Fred generally _____ where to go on vacation after he reads some travel books.
   b. As a matter of fact, Fred makes all his _____ after he reads books or magazines.

inform *(v.)*
information *(n.)*

2. a. The Registrar's Office _____ students when they are accepted to a college.
   b. The Office of Admissions mails this _____ to the students

react *(v.)*
reaction *(n.)*

3. a. John _____ strongly when he is surprised. He never says anything, or shows any feelings.
   b. His _____ are not usually easy to see.

protect *(v.)*
protection *(n.)*

4. a. An umbrella _____ you from the rain when the wind is blowing very hard.
   b. On rainy and windy days, a raincoat gives better _____ than an umbrella does.

adopt *(v.)*
adoption *(n.)*

5. a. When a couple _____ a child, the entire family is usually very happy.
   b. Before the _____ takes place, the whole family usually discusses the decision together.

In English, the noun form and the verb form of some words are the same, for example, *visit* (v.), *visit* (n.). Complete each sentence with the correct form of the words on the left. In addition, indicate whether you are using the verb *(v.)* or the noun *(n.)* form of each word. **Write all the verbs in the simple present tense. They may be affirmative or negative. The nouns may be singular or plural.**

plan

1. a. Terry has several _____ for his career.
      (v., n.)

   b. For example, he _____ to move to another
      (v., n.)
      city and to work for the government.

care

2. a. All parents give love and _____ to their children.
      (v., n.)

   b. In happy families, parents and children _____
      (v., n.)
      about each other very much.

record

3. a. The Records Office at City Hall keeps all the
      _____ of births, marriages, and deaths.
      (v., n.)

   b. However, the Records Office _____ sales of
      property. The City Real Estate   *(v., n.)*
      Office keeps all that information on file.

search

4. a. When I lose my car keys, I usually _____ for
      them in my pockets.   *(v., n.)*

   b. Sometimes my _____ is not successful, so I
      (v., n.)
      look for my keys on the floor.

worry

5. a. Lee has many _____ about his family.
      (v., n.)

   b. However, he _____ about unimportant matters.
      (v., n.)

Another Look

Read this adoptive mother's journal entry. Then answer the questions which follow.

Diary of an Adoptive Mother

January 1: It has happened, I got a call today saying a little girl in Russia is now my little girl. There is a lot of paperwork to do, and we have to travel to Russia to bring her home, but now it is certain. I think I'll tell some close friends. Jason is so excited. I haven't told Steven yet. How can I tell a seven-year-old that he has a sister who is already five years old?

January 10: Today I received a picture of Katerina. The picture is small and not very clear, but I look at it over and over again. I don't know anything else about her. She has lived in an orphanage for most of her life. I wonder how I will talk to her. I don't speak Russian, and she doesn't speak English.

February 1: Today I showed Katerina's picture to Steven. He is very happy and wants to tell all his friends about his new sister. I want to buy some clothes for Katerina, but I don't know her size. I haven't received any more information from the adoption agency, and I'm feeling a little worried.

February 16: Finally! Today we received good news! All the papers are ready and tomorrow we will go to Russia to bring Katerina home with us.

February 18: Today I met my daughter for the first time. She is very small, very thin, and very afraid. On the way home in the airplane, she slept most of the time. When she woke up, she cried. I am very nervous and hope that I can be a good mother to Katerina.

February 19: Steven met his sister this morning. Although Katerina was shy at first, soon she and Steven began to communicate in a mixture of Russian, English, and hand gestures. Steven and his sister get along well together. In fact, he is able to help her communicate with Jason and me. I am worried about how Katerina will be in school. Next week she will start kindergarten. How will she communicate with the other children? How will she understand her teacher?

March 21: Katerina looks much healthier now. She has gained weight, her hair is shiny, and her skin is clear. She loves to watch television with her brother, and she has learned to roller-skate. She is doing well in school, and her English gets better every day. Although she sometimes looks sad, and sometimes cries, most of the time she is happy. I think she is slowly getting used to her new life with us. After only three months, I can't imagine my life without her.

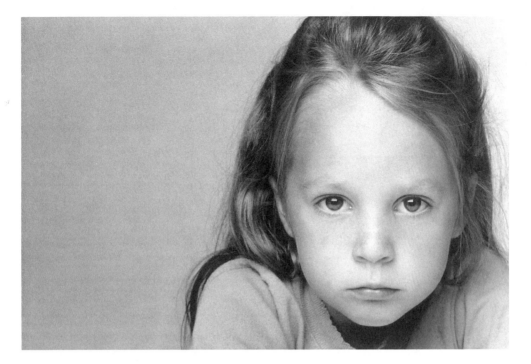

QUESTIONS FOR ANOTHER LOOK

1. Who is the writer of this diary? _____

2. Who is Katerina?
   a. The adoptive mother
   b. The adoptive father
   c. The adopted child

3. Who is Jason?
   a. The adoptive mother
   b. The adoptive father
   c. The adopted child

4. Who is Steven?
   a. The adoptive father
   b. The writer's son
   c. The adopted child

5. In the last sentence of the story, the writer says, "After only three months, I can't image my life without her." What does this sentence mean?
   a. The writer is happy that she has adopted Katerina.
   b. The writer is not happy that she has adopted Katerina.

1. Read the following chart and answer the questions that follow.

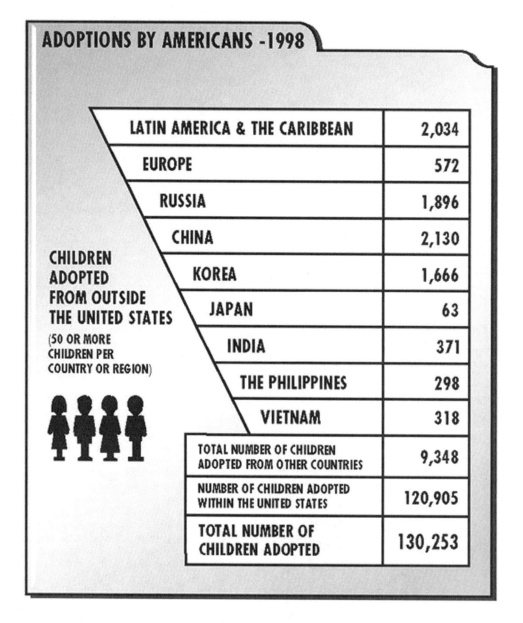

ADOPTIONS BY AMERICANS -1998

LATIN AMERICA & THE CARIBBEAN	2,034
EUROPE	572
RUSSIA	1,896
CHINA	2,130
KOREA	1,666
JAPAN	63
INDIA	371
THE PHILIPPINES	298
VIETNAM	318
TOTAL NUMBER OF CHILDREN ADOPTED FROM OTHER COUNTRIES	9,348
NUMBER OF CHILDREN ADOPTED WITHIN THE UNITED STATES	120,905
TOTAL NUMBER OF CHILDREN ADOPTED	130,253

CHILDREN ADOPTED FROM OUTSIDE THE UNITED STATES

(50 OR MORE CHILDREN PER COUNTRY OR REGION)

a. Where are the greatest number of children adopted from?
   1. From other countries
   2. From Latin America and the Caribbean
   3. From inside the United States

b. Of all the children who are adopted by Americans, what percent are adopted from outside the United States?
   1. 14%
   2. 50%
   3. 86%

c. Of all the children who are adopted by Americans, what percent are adopted from inside the United States?
   1. 14%
   2. 50%
   3. 86%

d. What are some reasons Americans adopt children from other countries? What do you think?

   _____

   _____

   _____

4. Work with another student.

   Student A: You are an adoptee. You were adopted when you were six months old. You are meeting your biological mother for the first time.

   Student B: You are Student A's natural mother/father. You are meeting your biological child for the first time since he/she was six months old.

   Write a dialogue. Introduce yourselves to each other. Then have a conversation. What will you say to each other? What questions will you ask each other? Share your dialogue with the class.

3. Work with a partner. Imagine that you want to adopt a child. What kind of child do you want? Describe the child's age, race, sex, etc. Why do you want to adopt this particular kind of child? What kind of life do you want for your adopted child?

I. Topics FOR *Discussion* AND *Writing*

1. Is adoption common in your country? Why or why not?

2. Do you think it is a good idea for adoptees to search for their birth parents? Explain your answer.

3. Do you think it is a good idea for people to adopt children who are a different race? Explain your answer.

4. In your country, can anyone adopt a child? For example, can a single man adopt a child? Do you think it is a good idea for anyone—male, female, married or single—to adopt a child? Explain your answer.

5. People sometimes give up their children for adoption. Imagine that you are going to give up your child. Write a letter to your best friend and explain your reasons.

6. **Write in your journal.** Imagine that you are married, and you cannot have children of your own. Will you adopt children? If you will, why is it important for you to have children? If you won't, explain your reasons.

Word Search

Read the words listed below. Find them in the puzzle and circle them. They may be written in any direction.

adoption	decision	protect	sealed
care	history	react	search
confidential	information	record	worthwhile

```
L  J  R  Z  W  S  N  R  D  L  S  N  E  C  R
A  F  W  V  O  S  W  O  W  B  M  U  G  B  U
I  N  F  O  R  M  A  T  I  O  N  E  Q  R  R
T  H  I  S  T  O  R  Y  T  T  L  D  R  E  K
N  G  F  R  H  C  D  H  J  S  P  U  C  A  J
E  Z  C  U  W  D  E  C  I  S  I  O  N  C  C
D  E  R  B  H  M  S  T  R  W  R  A  D  T  N
I  S  K  P  I  K  T  D  O  D  S  L  J  A  M
F  S  E  A  L  E  D  Q  Y  R  V  Y  T  Y  I
N  G  R  A  E  P  U  J  E  A  P  T  Z  S  J
O  C  V  H  R  X  F  Z  W  L  V  V  R  B  Z
C  Z  H  Q  T  C  R  B  L  G  I  Q  F  S  M
C  B  K  Q  M  O  H  K  W  R  M  R  Z  J  D
```

Crossword Puzzle

Read the clues on the next page. Write the answers in the correct spaces in the puzzle.

Crossword Puzzle Clues

Across Clues

1. I ate my food, and the dog ate _____ food.
5. _____ means make a child part of your family.
7. Response
8. I didn't eat anything all day. _____, I'm very hungry now.
12. The time before something happens
15. White, black, Asian: each one is a _____.
16. At the present time
18. Adopted children
19. Closed; no one can see.
21. Two people, usually a man and a woman
22. I have my books, and they have _____ books.
23. I didn't sleep well last night. I am _____ tired.

Down Clues

1. Babies
2. Make up your own mind about something
3. She likes her teacher. He likes _____ teacher, too.
4. Secret
6. We all have _____ own homes.
9. The opposite of **no**
10. Valuable
11. Look for
13. Biological mother and father
14. Records; important papers
17. She lost _____ bag.
20. You passed _____ test!
21. Parents _____ about their children.

I	she	they
me	her	them
my	her	their

Read the passage below. Complete each blank space with one of the pronouns listed above. You may use the pronouns more than once.

Naturally, adopted children have different feelings about

_____ birth parents. Many adoptees want to search for
     (1)

_____, but others do not. _____ have different feel-
    (2)   (3)

ings. Jake says, " _____ don't think _____ will ever
            (4)   (5)

search out _____ birth mother. _____ might want
       (6)   (7)

to get some more facts, but _____ don't feel _____
          (8)   (9)

really want to go looking." Carla was adopted when _____ was
              (10)

four years old. _____ adoptive parents also adopted another lit-
     (11)

tle girl. Carla says, "Sometimes _____ sister and
          (12)

_____ will talk. _____ says _____
  (13)   (14)   (15)

doesn't want to look for _____ birth mother when
        (16)

_____ gets older, but _____ have mixed feelings.
  (17)   (18)

Sometimes _____ feel that _____ want to look for
      (19)   (20)

_____, and _____ mother says _____
  (21)   (22)   (23)

will help _____ when _____ am older."
     (24)   (25)

1. Some twins do not grow up together because they live with different families. Sometimes these twins are adopted separately. Is this a good idea? Explain your answer.

2. Some families have adopted children in addition to their own biological children. Do you think they are treated differently by the parents? Explain your answer.

1. When a couple has twins or triplets, how does their life change? What problems may occur?

2. Read the following statements then watch the video once or twice. Check whether they are true (T) or false (F). If the statement is false, rewrite it so that it is true.

____ T ____ F   1. Homes with triplets are quiet places to live.

_____

____ T ____ F   2. In the video, the first set of triplets is 14 months old.

_____

____ T ____ F   3. The triplets are independent of their parents.

_____

____ T ____ F   4. The Ferrantes had triplets a few months after they adopted a baby.

_____

____ T ____ F   5. Some of the parents don't get as much help from other people now as they did when their children were younger.

_____

3. Discuss with a partner or group. Are there advantages to having three children at once? If so, what are they?

Surfing THE **INTERNET**

Use a search engine, such as Netscape, Yahoo, Google, or Excite. Type in "identical triplets" and read one or two stories about them. What did you find out. Discuss your information with a partner or small group.

Optional Activity: Enter the key words "parenting" and "twins" or "triplets" into a search engine. What advice is given to parents of twins and triplets? Print out and read the information. With a group discuss the advice you would give to the parents in the video "Raising Triplets."

UNIT 3

TECHNOLOGY IN OUR EVERYDAY LIVES

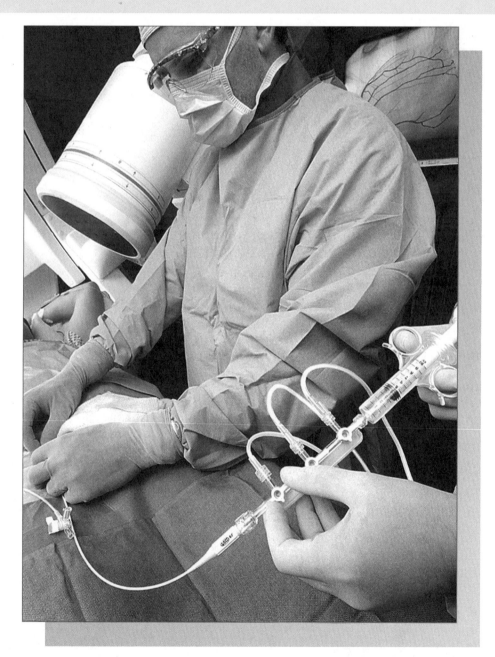

5

Laptops for the Classroom

Prereading Preparations

1. Look at the photograph. What is the student using?

   a. a calculator

   b. a laptop

   c. a typewriter

2. Do you have one of these? If so, what do you use it for?

3. What are the advantages of such a device?

4. Work with one or two partners. Make a list of the people who might use this device, and the uses they might have for it.

People	How Would They Use It?

Laptops for the Classroom

1   Laptop computers are popular all over the world. People use them on trains and airplanes, in airports and hotels. These laptops connect people to their workplace. In the United States today, laptops also connect students to their classrooms. Westlake College in Virginia is the 10th school across the country to

5   join IBM ThinkPad University. ThinkPad University is a laptop computer program that allows students to do schoolwork anywhere they want.

Beginning this fall, Westlake College will give portable PCs,[1] or laptops, to each new student. Within five years, each of the other 1,500 students at the college will receive a laptop, too. The laptops are part of a $10 million computer

10   program at Westlake, a 110-year-old college. The students with laptops will also have access to the Internet. In addition, they will be able to use e-mail to "speak" with their teachers, their classmates, and their families. However, the most important part of the laptop program is that students will be able to use computers without going to computer labs. They can work with it at home, in a

15   fast-food restaurant or under the trees—anywhere at all!

IBM started its ThinkPad program at Minnesota College three years ago. The computer giant hopes to double the number of schools using laptops to 20 in the near future. Because of the many changes in computer technology, laptop use in higher education, such as colleges and universities, is workable. As

20   laptops become more powerful, they become more similar to desktop computers. In addition, the portable PCs can connect students to not only the Internet, but also libraries and other resources. State higher-education officials are studying how laptops can help students. State officials also are testing laptop programs at other universities, too.

25   At Westlake College, more than 60 percent of the faculty use computers. The laptops will allow all teachers to use computers in their lessons. As one Westlake teacher said, "Here we are in the middle of Virginia and we're giving students a window on the world. They can see everything and do everything."

[1]PC: a personal computer; also called a desktop computer.

Fact-Finding Exercise

Read the passage once. Then read the following statements. Check whether they are True (T) or False (F). If a statement is false, change the statement so that it is true. Then go back to the passage and find the line that supports your answer.

1. _____ True _____ False   ThinkPad University is a college.

    _____

2. _____ True _____ False   Westlake College is a new school.

    _____

3. _____ True _____ False   Westlake College will give each new student a laptop computer.

    _____

4. _____ True _____ False   Students with laptops can only do school-work at college.

    _____

5. _____ True _____ False   Laptops can connect students to libraries and to the Internet.

    _____

6. _____ True _____ False   In the future, 20 schools will use laptops for all their students.

    _____

PART 1

Skim through the passage. Then read the following statements. Choose the one that is the correct main idea of the reading.

a. Westlake College has more than 1,500 students.

b. New Westlake College students will receive laptop computers to use for their schoolwork.

c. ThinkPad University will connect students to their classroom using laptop computers in 20 schools.

Scan the passage. Work with a partner to fill in the flowchart below with information from the reading.

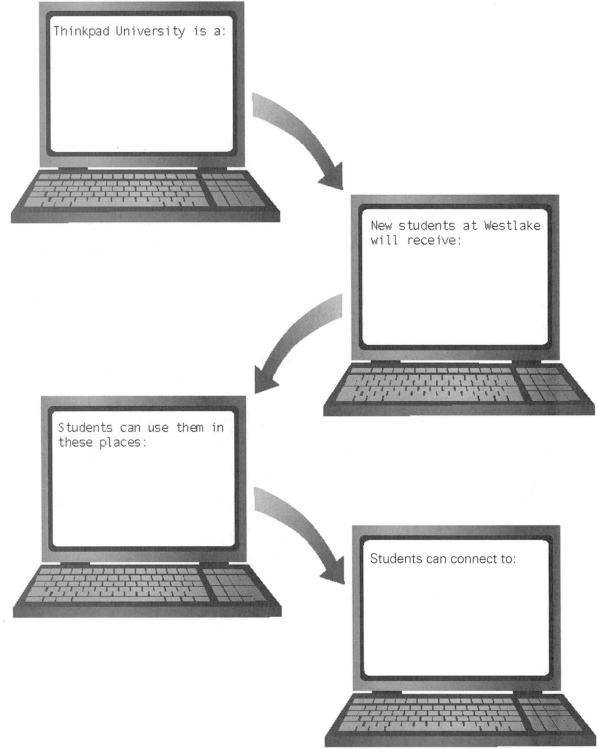

Thinkpad University is a:

New students at Westlake will receive:

Students can use them in these places:

Students can connect to:

Reading Analysis

Read each question carefully. Either circle the letter of the correct answer, or write your answer in the space provided.

1. **Beginning this fall,** Westlake College will give **portable PCs,** or laptops, to each new student.

   a. **Beginning this fall** means
      1. starting in September
      2. starting in January
      3. starting next semester

   b. **Portable PCs** are
      1. home computers
      2. classrooms
      3. laptops

   c. **Portable** means
      1. you can work on it
      2. you can carry it
      3. you can buy it

2. **In addition,** they will be able to use **e-mail** to **"speak"** with their teachers, classmates, and their families.

   a. **In addition** means
      1. however
      2. also
      3. maybe

   b. To use **e-mail** means to communicate by
      1. telephone
      2. writing letters
      3. computer

   c. Why is **"speak"** in quotation marks?
      1. They don't really talk
      2. It's a new word
      3. It's a difficult word

3. Read the following sentences: However, the most important part of the laptop program is that students will be able to use computers without going to computer labs. They can work with it at home, in a fast-food restaurant or under the trees—**anywhere at all!**

a. Do students have to go to computer labs to use laptops?

  1. Yes
  2. No

b. Where can students use them?

   _____

c. **Anywhere at all** means

  1. a few places
  2. all places
  3. some places

4. Read the following sentences: IBM started its ThinkPad program at Minnesota College three years ago. **The computer giant** hopes to **double** the number of schools using laptops to 20 in the near future.

a. What does **the computer giant** mean?

  1. Minnesota College
  2. IBM
  3. Westlake College

b. How many schools use laptops now?

  1. 10
  2. 20
  3. 30

5. Read the following sentence: Because of the many changes in computer technology, laptop use in **higher education, such as** colleges and universities, is **workable.**

a. What are examples of **higher education?**

   _____

b. What does **such as** mean?

  1. Also
  2. For example
  3. Except

c. **Workable** means
      1. possible
      2. difficult
      3. expensive

6. The portable PCs can connect students to **not only** the Internet, **but also** libraries and other resources.

   Not only . . . but also means

   a. and . . . also
   b. but . . . not
   c. only . . . if

7. Read the following sentence: Here we are in the middle of Virginia and we're giving students **a window on the world.**

   a. **A window on the world** means that students
      1. can travel around the world
      2. can see the world
      3. can get information from around the world

   b. How are the teachers giving students **a window on the world?**
      1. By giving them laptops
      2. By teaching them about the world
      3. By giving them good lessons

D. *Think* About It

Read the following questions and think about the answers. Write your answer below each question. Then compare your answers with those of your classmates.

1. People use laptop computers on trains and airplanes, and in airports and hotels, to connect them to their workplace. Why do you think people need to be connected to their workplace?

   _____

   _____

   _____

2. E-mail lets students "speak" to their families. Why might this be important?

   _____

   _____

   _____

3. IBM is a big computer company. Why do you think they started the ThinkPad program in colleges?

   _____

   _____

   _____

E. DICTIONARY SKILLS

Read the dictionary entry for each word, and think about the context of the sentence. Write the number of the appropriate definition on the line next to the word. In addition, circle *noun, verb,* or *adjective* where indicated. Then choose the sentence with the correct answer.

1.

> **allow** *v.* **1** to let, permit: *We allowed our son to use the family car.* **2** to agree reluctantly, *(syn.)* to **concede:** *The witness allowed that he had not told the complete truth. -adj.* **allowable.**

ThinkPad University is a laptop computer program that **allows** students to do schoolwork anywhere they want. The laptops will **allow** all teachers to use computers in their lessons.

a. **allow:** _____

b. 1. ThinkPad University is a laptop computer program that agrees reluctantly with students to do schoolwork anywhere they want.

   2. ThinkPad University is a laptop computer program that lets students do schoolwork anywhere they want.

2.

> **program** *n.* **1** any organized plan to accomplish a goal: *Many government programs, such as mortgage interest deduction, help the wealthy.* **2** a television or radio show: *All the news programs include weather reports.* **3** a written schedule of events such as for a church, sports, or theatrical event: *All the actors' names were listed in the program.* **4** a set of coded instructions telling a computer how to process information:
>
> *This program lets you make three-dimensional drawings on your computer.* —*v.* **-grammed, -gramming, -grams 1** to make up a schedule, include s.t. in a program: *An organizer programmed meetings for a conference.* **2** to write a set of instructions for a computer: *She knows how to program in several computer languages.* **3** to give instructions to a computer: *I programmed my VCR to tape-record the football game.*

ThinkPad University is a laptop computer **program** that allows students to do schoolwork anywhere they want.

a. **program:** _____ (noun/verb)

b. 1. ThinkPad University is a laptop computer organized plan to accomplish the goal of allowing students to do schoolwork anywhere they want.

   2. ThinkPad University is a laptop computer television show that allows students to do schoolwork anywhere they want.

   3. ThinkPad University is a laptop computer set of written instructions that allows students to do schoolwork anywhere they want.

3.

> **access** _v._ to get into s.t., enter: _He accessed the computer program by typing in the correct access code._ -_n._ [U] **1** entrance, permission to use: _I got access to the library by showing my identity card._ **2** a way or means of reaching or entering a place: _The only access to the island is by boat or plane._ -_adj._ related to entering: _This is your access code for the computer._ || _Please use the access road behind the building._

The students with laptops will also have **access** to the Internet.

a. **access:** _____ (verb/noun/adjective)

b. 1. The students with laptops will also have a way to enter the Internet.

2. The students with laptops will also have permission for the Internet.

4.

> **giant** _n._ **1** a person, animal, plant, or object much larger than normal: _This tomato plant is a giant._ **2** (in fairy stories) an imaginary person who is very big and strong **3** _fig._ a very big company: _IBM is a giant in the computer industry._ -_adj._ much larger than normal: _The giant redwood trees in California are very beautiful._

IBM, the computer **giant,** hopes to double the number of schools using laptops.

a. **giant:** _____ (noun/adjective)

b. 1. IBM, the computer object that is much larger than normal, hopes to double the number of schools using laptops.

2. IBM, the imaginary computer company, hopes to double the number of schools using laptops.

3. IBM, the very big computer company, hopes to double the number of schools using laptops.

5.

> **popular** *adj.* **1** well-liked, admired by a group of people: *She is very popular with her college classmates.* **2** having widespread acceptance: *The Mercedes automobile is popular among the rich.* **3** typical of the interests of ordinary people: *Soap operas and country music are forms of popular entertainment.* *-adv.* **popularly.**

Laptop computers are **popular** all over the world. People use them on trains and airplanes, in airports and hotels.

a. **popular:** _____

b. 1. Laptop computers are typical of ordinary people's interest all over the world. People use them on trains and airplanes, in airports and hotels.

2. Laptop computers have widespread acceptance all over the world. People use them on trains and airplanes, in airports and hotels.

3. Laptop computers are admired by people all over the world. People use them on trains and airplanes, in airports and hotels.

In English, the noun form and the verb form of some words are the same, for example, *test (v.)*, *test (n.)*. Complete each sentence with the correct form of the word on the left. Circle (*v.*) if you are using the verb, or (*n.*) if you are using the noun form of each word. **Write all the verbs in the simple present tense. They may be affirmative or negative. The nouns may be singular or plural.**

program

1. a. Winnie wants to lose weight, so she has joined a
      weight-loss _____ .
                          (v., n.)

   b. A weight-loss consultant _____ special activities
                                       (v., n.)
      and classes for her clients to help them exercise and
      eat less.

access

2. a. Faye usually _____ her e-mail account in the
                          (v., n.)
      morning because she has time to write back to anyone
      who contacted her.

   b. As a student, I have _____ to the library, the cafe-
      teria, and the gym.   (v., n.)

e-mail

3. a. David is studying in another country now, but he can
      receive _____ at the college.
                   (v., n.)

   b. I _____ David very often, but he would like me to.
        (v., n.)

hope

4. a. William _____ he will be admitted to Manhattan University. *(v., n.)*

    b. William has only applied to one university. He has put all of his _____ into this one school.
        (v., n.)

use

5. a. I don't get a lot of _____ out of my bicycle. I don't ride it very often. *(v., n.)*

    b. If I _____ it more often, I am going to sell it.
        (v., n.)

Read the following description of today's banking services. Then answer the questions which follow.

Banking at Home

Many people dislike walking to the bank, standing in long lines, and running out of checks. They are dissatisfied with their bank's limited hours, too. They want to do some banking at night, and on weekends. For such people, their problems may soon be over. Before long, they may be able to do their banking from the comfort of their own home, any hour of the day, any day of the week.

Many banks are preparing "online branches," or Internet offices, which means that people will be able to take care of much of their banking business through their home computers. This process is called interactive banking. At these online branches, customers will be able to view all their accounts, move money between accounts, apply for a loan, and get current information on products such as credit cards. Customers will also be able to pay their bills electronically, and even e-mail questions to the bank.

Banks are creating online services for several reasons. One reason is that banks must compete for customers, who will switch to another bank if they are dissatisfied with the service they receive. The convenience of online banking appeals to the kind of customer banks most want to keep—people who are young, well-educated, and have good incomes. Banks also want to take advantage of modern technology as they move into the twenty-first century.

Online banking may not be appropriate for everyone. For instance, many people do not have computers at home. Other people prefer to go to the bank and handle their accounts the traditional way. Even though online banking may never completely replace a walk-in bank, it is a service that many customers are going to want to use.

QUESTIONS FOR ANOTHER LOOK

1. What are some reasons why people are unhappy with having to go to the bank?
   a. They don't like to walk there.
   b. They don't like to talk on the phone.
   c. They want to bank on Sundays.
   d. They want to do their banking in the evening.
   e. They don't have a lot of money.

2. In the future, some people will bank at home with:

   _____

3. Interactive banking is
   a. banking through the Internet
   b. banking in your office
   c. banking at the bank

4. a. In the story, what kind of customer will use "online banking" in the future?

   _____

   b. Why do banks want that kind of customer?
      1. Because they have good jobs
      2. Because they have a lot of money

5. What is a reason why people may **not** want to use "online banking?"
   a. Some people don't have computers at home.
   b. Some people like to bank on weekends.

1. Go to your bank or another local bank. Find out what online services the bank offers. Report back to your class.

2. Visit the computer center/computer lab in your school. Find out what computers and computer systems are available to students. Report back to your class.

I. Topics FOR *Discussion* AND *Writing*

1. ThinkPad University is a laptop computer program that allows students to do schoolwork anywhere they want. Work with one or two partners. Make a list of the advantages and the disadvantages of students working wherever they want. Compare your list with your classmates' lists. Are there more advantages or more disadvantages to this type of program? Take a vote in class. Do most of your classmates like or dislike this type of computer program?

2. Describe other ways that computers make people's lives easier or more convenient.

3. **Write in your journal.** One of the consequences of ThinkPad University and online banking is that people can do much of their schoolwork and banking by themselves. As a result, they may have less interaction with other people. Do you think this is a positive or a negative outcome, or effect, of modern technology? Write your opinion, and explain why you think this way.

Read the words listed below. Find them in the puzzle and circle them. They may be written in any direction.

access	connect	giant	program
colleges	education	popular	technology
computer	future	portable	universities

```
S  E  I  T  I  S  R  E  V  I  N  U  K  F  D
R  P  T  C  E  N  N  O  C  E  E  S  D  U  I
N  O  I  T  A  C  U  D  E  A  S  G  X  R  H
C  R  N  Z  U  H  H  J  E  S  H  S  G  L  I
F  T  G  P  F  M  E  N  E  J  A  O  Z  A  E
M  A  R  G  O  R  P  C  O  M  P  U  T  E  R
N  B  N  V  U  P  C  O  L  L  E  G  E  S  J
B  L  V  T  K  A  U  X  G  G  O  T  S  E  Z
Y  E  U  N  Z  G  A  L  M  Z  Y  G  N  I  K
J  F  J  A  W  N  D  Q  A  S  V  Y  Y  B  D
O  U  X  I  D  B  C  L  Q  R  N  X  F  X  Q
N  A  E  G  H  J  S  F  F  W  O  Q  C  V  D
```

Crossword Puzzle

Read the clues on the next page. Write the answers in the correct spaces in the puzzle.

Crossword Puzzle Clues

Across Clues

3. Not happy; not content

6. April, _____, June, July

7. Permit

9. The teachers at a college are its _____.

14. The _____ is a system of computers connected all around the world.

17. The past tense of **sit**

18. A personal computer

22. Something _____ is something that has widespread acceptance.

25. A school of higher education

26. The past tense of **hit**

27. I, _____; he, him

28. I haven't eaten dinner _____. It's only 4 o'clock.

Down Clues

1. A _____ is a portable computer.

2. The opposite of **on**

3. The opposite of **night**

4. John felt happy, _____ he smiled.

5. _____ is a way to send letters electronically.

7. I have _____ to an electronic library through my personal computer.

8. A personal computer

10. Class begins _____ 9 o'clock.

11. The opposite of **no**

12. A very large company, such as General Motors or Toyota

13. The opposite of **off**

15. We have _____ study every day.

16. The past tense of **do**

19. I use a _____ to open my mailbox.

20. A _____ is an organized plan to accomplish a goal.

21. We _____ studying English.

23. The opposite of **on time**

24. When I am on the Internet, I am _____.

Grammar Cloze Quiz

Read the passage below. Complete each blank space with one of the prepositions listed below. You may use prepositions more than once.

at	in	on	over	to

Laptop computers are popular all _____ the world. People
                                        (1)
use them _____ trains and airplanes, _____ airports
              (2)   (3)
and hotels. These laptops connect people _____ their workplace.
                                                  (4)
_____ the United States today, laptops also connect students
      (5)
_____ their classrooms. Westlake College _____
      (6)   (7)
Virginia is the 10th school _____ the country to join IBM
                                  (8)
ThinkPad University. IBM started its ThinkPad program _____ the
                                                            (9)
Minnesota College three years ago. The computer giant hopes to double the
number of schools _____ the near future.
                        (10)

A New Way to Go

Prereading Preparation

Look at the photograph. This is a picture of a "Segway." Work with a partner and answer the questions below.

1. How many people can ride on it? _____

2. How fast do you think it goes? _____

3. Where can it be useful? _____

4. Who might it be useful for? _____

5. Why might it be useful? _____

6. How does the Segway get power?
   a. From an engine
   b. From batteries
   c. From the person riding on it

7. How much does a Segway cost? What do you think?
   a. $200
   b. $1,000
   c. $8,000

A New Way to Go

1   It looks like a scooter, but it travels 15 miles per hour (24 kilometers per hour). It uses two batteries and only ten cents of electricity a day. It can go backwards or forwards, and it never falls over. It doesn't have brakes, but it knows when to stop. What is it? It is a "Segway," and Dean Kamen invented it. It

5   costs $8,000.
     Right now, only a few people use the Segway scooter. This electric scooter is very easy to use and can go in any direction. You can control it with your body. For example, when you move to the left, the scooter moves to the left. When you tilt forward, it goes straight ahead. In some states in the United States, such as

10   New Hampshire and Florida, post office workers use Segways to deliver the mail. The scooters help the workers do their work more easily. In some cities, such as Boston and Atlanta, police officers use them to travel on crowded streets.
     Dean Kamen believes that many other people will soon ride Segways. The

15   scooters weigh about 65 pounds (about 29½ kilograms). They are cheaper than cars, and they are faster than walking. Cars are useful for long distances. But for short distances, electric scooters can be very useful. They are good for the environment, too. They only use a little electricity and do not cause air pollution like cars do. Dean Kamen believes that our lives will be a little easier with his

20   invention.
     Before he invented the Segway, Dean Kamen worked on medical projects. When his brother was in medical school, he needed an easier way to give medicine to some patients. Dean's brother discussed this problem with him. Dean invented a special machine so that patients do not have to take medicine

25   by mouth. Doctors can give them medicine through their skin. Now, many doctors and hospitals use this machine.

In addition to the Segway, Dean Kamen has invented another device to make life easier. It is a new kind of wheelchair to help people who cannot walk. This wheelchair can climb curbs. It can "walk" up stairs, too. It can travel over rocks and sand. This new wheelchair can even raise itself up so that the person in this wheelchair can reach something on a high shelf. It can go up to the height of a standing person.

Dean Kamen wants to help as many people as possible with his inventions, and wants to encourage other people to invent useful devices, too.

Fact-Finding Exercise

Read the passage once. Then read the following statements. Check whether they are True or False. If a statement is false, change the statement so that it is true. Then go back to the passage and find the line that supports your answer.

1. _____ True _____ False   The Segway uses a lot of electricity.

_____

2. _____ True _____ False   The scooter is helpful for postal workers and police officers.

_____

3. _____ True _____ False   Cars can cause air pollution.

_____

4. _____ True _____ False   Scooters can be useful for long distances.

_____

5. _____ True _____ False   Some doctors use Dean's other machine to give medicine to their patients.

_____

6. _____ True _____ False   The new wheelchair is helpful for postal workers and police officers.

_____

7. _____ True _____ False   The new wheelchair travels 15 miles per hour.

_____

Skimming and Scanning Exercise

PART 1

Skim through the passage. Then read the following statements. Choose the one that is the correct main idea of the reading.

    a. The new wheelchair can be very helpful because it climbs stairs and travels over rocks and sand.

    b. Segways can be important to the environment because they do not cause air pollution.

    c. Dean Kamen has invented many things that can make life easier for many different people.

PART 2

Scan the passage. Work with a partner to complete the following chart.

Dean Kamen's Inventions		
What is the invention?	Segway	
Who is it helpful for?		
Why is it helpful?		

Read each question carefully. Either circle the letter of the correct answer or write your answer in the space provided.

1. A Segway can go **backwards** or **forwards,** and it never falls over. **Backwards** and **forwards** are

   a. synonyms

   b. antonyms

   c. numbers

2. This electric scooter is very easy to use, and can go in any **direction.** You can control it with your body. For example, when you move to the left, the scooter moves to the left. When you tilt forward, it goes straight ahead.

   a. **Direction** means

      1. way

      2. speed

      3. road

   b. What directions can the electric scooter go?

      _____

3. Segways are cheaper than cars, and they are faster than walking.

   a. Cars are

      1. more expensive than Segways

      2. the same price as Segways

      3. less expensive than Segways

   b. Walking is

      1. faster than a Segway

      2. slower than a Segway

      3. easier than a Segway

4. Segways are good for the environment. Write two reasons.

   1. _____

   2. _____

5. Dean's brother needed an easier way to give medicine to some **patients.**
   Dean invented a special machine so that patients do not have to take
   medicine by mouth. Doctors can give them medicine through their skin.

   a. **Patients** are
      1. people who work in a hospital
      2. people who study to become doctors
      3. people who are sick in a hospital

   b. It is easier for patients to take medicine
      1. through their skin
      2. by mouth

6. The new wheelchairs can climb **curbs. Curbs** are on
   a. stairs
   b. streets
   c. sidewalks

7. Dean Kamen wants to help as many people as possible with his **inventions,** and wants to encourage other people to invent things too.
   Inventions are things you
   a. make
   b. find
   c. ride

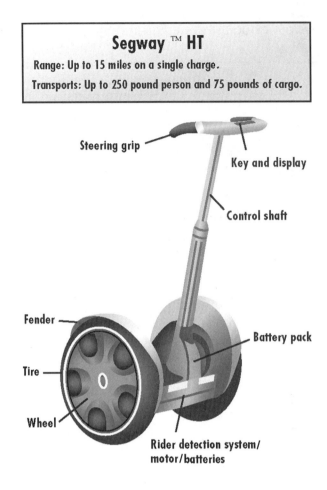

Segway ™ HT

Range: Up to 15 miles on a single charge.

Transports: Up to 250 pound person and 75 pounds of cargo.

Steering grip

Key and display

Control shaft

Fender

Battery pack

Tire

Wheel

Rider detection system/
motor/batteries

D. *Think* About It

Read the following questions and think about the answers. Write your answers below each question. Then, compare your answers with those of your classmates.

1. Why don't many people have Segways?

   _____

2. Why is it important that the new wheelchairs reach the height of a standing person?

   _____

3. Why do many doctors and hospitals use Dean Kamen's medical invention?

   _____

E. DICTIONARY SKILLS

Read the dictionary entry for each word, and think about the context of the sentence. Write the number of the appropriate definition on the line next to the word. Then choose the sentence with the correct answer.

Dean Kamen has invented another **device** to make life easier. It is a new kind of wheelchair to help people who cannot walk. This wheelchair can climb curbs. It can "walk" up stairs, too. This new wheelchair can even raise itself up so that the person in this wheelchair can reach something on a high shelf. Dean Kamen wants to help as many people as possible with his inventions and wants to encourage other people to invent new **devices** that are **useful**, too.

1.

> **de-vice** *n.* **1** an electrical or mechanical machine: *The computer is an electronic device.* **2** a tool or implement: *An electric can opener is also a device.* **3** a trick or secret means to an end: *His outbursts of anger are just a device to move everyone's attention from his guilt.* **4 to leave to one's own devices:** to leave s.o. alone without help or interference.

a. **device:** _____

b. 1. Dean Kamen has invented another mechanical machine to make life easier.

2. Dean Kamen has invented another trick to make life easier.

2.

> **use-ful** *adj.* **1** helpful, handy: *Tools such as a hammer and screwdriver, are useful when you want to fix something.* **2** valuable, worthwhile: *Her language skills make her a useful addition to our team.* *-adv.* **usefully;** *-n* [U] **usefulness.**

a. **useful:** _____

b. 1. Dean Kamen wants other people to invent new devices that are helpful.

2. Dean Kamen wants other people to invent new devices that are valuable.

PART 1

In English, some verbs become nouns by adding the suffix *-ion,* for example, *act (v.), action (n.).* Complete each sentence with the correct form of the words on the left. **Write all verbs in the simple present tense. They may be affirmative or negative. The nouns may be singular or plural.**

invent *(v.)*
invention *(n.)*

1. a. Dean Kamen's many _____ can be helpful for people.
    b. Some people _____ new products to make our lives easier.

pollute *(v.)*
pollution *(n.)*

2. a. Bicycles _____ the air of crowded cities.
    b. Today, many people are worried about air
        _____.

direct *(v.)*
direction *(n.)*

3. a. Teachers _____ their students to read each question carefully on an exam.
    b. The students read the _____ carefully so they won't make mistakes.

discuss *(v.)*
discussion *(n.)*

4. a. After we read a story in class, the teacher _____ it with the class.
    b. We had a very interesting _____ in class last week.

add *(v.)*
addition *(n.)*

5. a. Inventors _____ to the list of new inventions every year.
    b. Many of these wonderful _____ help people move about, live longer, and feel healthier.

In English, the noun form and the verb form of some words are the same, for example, *move (v.), move (n.)*. Complete each sentence with the correct form of the word on the left. Circle (v.) if you are using a verb, or *(n.)* if you are using a noun. **Write all the verbs in the simple present tense. They may be affirmative or negative. The nouns may be plural or singular.**

work

1. a. My sister _____ on Monday. She only goes to her
        (v. , n.)
        job on Saturdays and Sundays.

    b. My father does all his _____ in the evening.
        (v., n.)

travel

2. a. José _____ every year to visit his family in Mexico.
        (v., n.)

    b. _____ can be very expensive for a large family.
        (v., n.)

control

3. a. Postal workers _____ the Segways with their
        bodies.   (v., n.)

    b. The _____ of these electric scooters is easy
        (v., n.)   to learn.

help

4. a. Sometimes I need a little _____ with my homework.
        (v., n.)

    b. My older sister often _____ me when I ask her.
        (v., n.)

cause

5. a. There are many different _____ of pollution.
        (v., n.)

    b. Segways are good for the environment because they
        _____ air pollution.
        (v., n.)

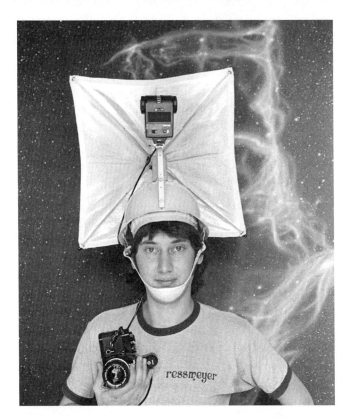

Read the following information about organizations that encourage young inventors. Then answer the questions that follow.

Young Inventors

Many organizations have contests to encourage young people to use their imaginations and make new inventions. The winners of the competitions receive prizes, usually money or scholarships for college. For example, last year, 12-year-old Jonathan Edwards was one of the winners of the Young Inventors Contest. This competition encourages students in elementary schools to use their imagination. Jonathan invented the Step Ramp. The Step Ramp is stairs that flatten down into a ramp. This special ramp can help people move heavy objects up the stairs. It can also be very useful for people in wheelchairs.

Ryan Patterson, who is 18 years old, won a $100,000 scholarship in the Westinghouse Science and Technology contest for his useful invention. It is a special glove, called the Sign Language Translator. People who are deaf and cannot speak sometimes use sign language. They use their hands to "speak."

When they wear Ryan's special glove, it translates sign language into words on a small computer screen. He hopes that his Sign Language Translator will be helpful and easy for many people to use.

Some contests also encourage young people to find ways to save energy. Every year, the U.S. Department of Energy has an "Energy Smart Schools" contest. Students can use their imaginations and their science knowledge. Michael Torrey, a fifth grader, invented a Miniature Hydroelectric Power Plant. This small device goes inside water pipes. Then, the device uses water to charge batteries, such as the batteries in a small radio. While someone is taking a shower or brushing their teeth, for example, the running water charges the batteries.

Jonathan Ioviero is a fifth grader, too. He invented the "Light Searcher." This device "looks" around the house. It can find lights that are on in empty rooms. Then it can turn the lights off. Both Michael's and Jonathan's devices are useful because they can help save energy. These young inventors can help people and the environment at the same time!

QUESTIONS FOR ANOTHER LOOK

1. Use the information in the story to complete the chart below.

Inventor's Name	Invention	What does it do?	Who can use it?

2. Which invention is the most useful? Why do you think so?

_____

1. Postal workers and police officers in some cities use Segways because they are helpful. Work in small groups. These electric scooters might be useful for other people, too. Make a list of these people, and write a reason why these scooters might be useful for them.

2. Work in a group. Think of an invention that people need. Describe your invention. Draw a picture of it if you can. Explain to the class why this invention is necessary or useful.

I. Topics FOR *Discussion* AND *Writing*

1. In what other places do you think electric scooters can be helpful? Why?

2. What do you think was the most important invention in the past? Why was this invention important? Write some reasons, and give examples.

3. What do you think might be an important invention in the future? Write about it. Describe what it might do and whom it might help.

4. **Write in your journal.** Think of a new invention that people need today. What will it do? Why will it be important? Who will be able to use it? How much might it cost?

Word Search

Read the words listed below. Find them in the puzzle and circle them. They may be written in any direction.

climb	deliver	encourage	pollution
control	direction	invention	scooter
crowded	electricity	machine	wheelchair

E N F E Q Y Z C A X B C M G Z

N L T X R U O I I I G R Z Z Y

N A E C J N T N D E L I V E R

Z O K C T H V W H P I W A C O

M R I R T E H N R C X H G I G

A C O T N R N O I T C E R I D

C L R T U N I L T C T E E T F

H U I O S L A C F Q C L G M C

I O H J W E L R I Y L C A D L

N O K Y B D E O W T H H R E D

E M B G S T E L P I Y A U E F

M W B N O D S D G W M I O O K

O X A O C J D Q J L S R C U R

O J C B M I L C W G L C N A L

K S X Q K G N Q C K S O E L I

Read the clues on the next page. Write the answers in the correct spaces in the puzzle.

Crossword Puzzle Clues

Across Clues

3. A place to buy stamps (2 words)

4. Not easy

5. The opposite of **forwards**

8. Create something new

9. The place where you go to learn

10. Lift something up

12. Everything around us

13. Helpful

16. Talk about

18. Sick people in a hospital

Down Clues

1. The opposite of **right**

2. This causes dirty air or water.

4. People who give medicine

5. We use these to stop a car.

6. Boston and Atlanta

7. People who protect us

11. New Hampshire and Florida

14. $29\frac{1}{2}$ kg = 65 _____

15. Not expensive

17. This covers your whole body.

Grammar Cloze Quiz

Read the passage below. Complete each blank space with one of the prepositions listed below. You may use the prepositions more than once.

by	on	through	up
in	over	to	with

Before he invented the Segway, Dean Kamen worked on medical projects. When his brother was _____ (1) medical school, he needed an easier way to give medicine _____ (2) some patients. Dean's brother discussed this problem _____ (3) him. Dean invented a special machine so that patients do not have to take medicine _____ (4) mouth. Doctors can give them medicine _____ (5) their skin. Now many doctors and hospitals use this machine.

In addition to the Segway, Dean Kamen has invented another thing to make life easier. It is a new kind of wheelchair. It can climb curbs and "walk" _____ (6) stairs, too. It can travel _____ (7) rocks and sand. This new wheelchair can even raise itself _____ (8) so that the person in this wheelchair can reach something _____ (9) a high shelf. It can go _____ (10) to the height of a standing person.

1. The two chapters in this unit describe many uses of modern technology and many technologically advanced products. In both chapters, computer technology is very important. How is computer technology important in our everyday lives?

2. Technology is an important part of our lives today. What are the advantages of modern technology? What the disadvantages?

VIDEO REPORT: Dean Kamen and the Segway

1. The video shows Dean Kamen and his invention, the Segway. Do you think the Segway will be as popular as the car or the laptop PC?

2. Read the questions then watch the video once or twice. Answer the questions alone, with a partner, or in a small group.

   a. How do riders control the Segway? How do they make it go forward and backward?

   b. Name two other inventions by Dean Kamen:

   c. Is the Segway safe? What happens if the Segway runs over someone's toes?

   d. Which of the following groups use the Segway?

Factory workers	Police
Postal Service workers	All of these

   e. How much will the Segway cost?

3. Discuss with your class: In the future, who will use the Segway? Where will Segways be used? Would you use one? How much would you be willing to pay for one?

 Surfing THE *INTERNET*

Enter the key words "young inventors" into a search engine such as Google, Yahoo, Excite, or MSN. What are some inventions children or teenagers have created? Print out a picture of the most interesting invention or description of the invention and report to your class.

Optional Activity: Read about Segway online at websites like the following: http://www.segway.com. Report the information that you learn to your classmates. For example, what kind of people and businesses use it?

UNIT 4

HEALTHY LIVING

The Dangers of Secondhand Smoke

Prereading Preparation

1. Look at the photograph. Describe what is happening. Is the man breathing in cigarette smoke, too?

2. What is secondhand smoke?

   a. It is smoke that the smoker breathes in from his own cigarette.
   b. It is smoke that a person breathes in when he smokes someone else's cigarette.
   c. It is smoke that a person breathes in when he is near a person who is smoking.

3. Is smoking harmful? Work with a partner, and list the reasons why you think smoking is or isn't harmful to smokers and to nonsmokers.

Is Smoking Harmful to Smokers?	Is Smoking Harmful to Nonsmokers?
Yes/No	Yes/No
Reasons:	**Reasons:**

The Dangers of Secondhand Smoke

Most people know that cigarette smoking is harmful to their health. Scientific research shows that it causes many kinds of diseases. In fact, many people who smoke get lung cancer. However, Edward Gilson has lung cancer, and he has never smoked cigarettes. He lives with his wife, Evelyn, who has smoked about a pack of cigarettes a day throughout their marriage. The Gilsons have been married for 35 years.

No one knows for sure why Mr. Gilson has lung cancer. Nevertheless, doctors believe that secondhand smoke may cause lung cancer in people who do not smoke because nonsmokers often breathe in the smoke from other people's cigarettes. This smoke is called secondhand smoke. Edward Gilson has been breathing this type of smoke for 35 years. Now he is dying of lung cancer. However, he is not alone. The U.S. Environmental Protection Agency[1] reports that about 53,000 people die in the United States each year as a result of exposure to secondhand smoke.

The smoke that comes from a lit cigarette contains many different poisonous chemicals. In the past, scientists did not think that these chemicals could harm a nonsmoker's health. Recently, though, scientists changed their opinion after they studied a large group of nonsmokers. They discovered that even nonsmokers had unhealthy amounts of these toxic chemicals in their bodies. As a matter of fact, almost all of us breathe tobacco smoke at times, whether we realize it or not. For example, we cannot avoid secondhand smoke in restaurants, hotels, and other public places. Even though many public places have nonsmoking areas, smoke flows in from the areas where smoking is permitted.

It is even harder for children to avoid secondhand smoke. In the United States, nine million children under the age of five live in homes with at least one smoker. Research shows that children who are exposed to secondhand smoke are sick more often than children who live in homes where no one smokes. The damaging effects of secondhand smoke on children also continue as they grow up. The children of smokers are more than twice as likely to develop lung cancer when they are adults as are children of nonsmokers. The risk is even higher for children who live in homes where both parents smoke.

---

[1]Environmental Protection Agency (EPA): A government department that is responsible for protecting the U.S. environment, particularly the air and water.

People are becoming very aware of the danger of secondhand smoke. As a result, they have passed laws that prohibit people from smoking in many public places. Currently, 45 states in the United States have laws that restrict, or limit, smoking. The most well-known law forbids people from smoking on domestic airline flights, i.e., flights within the country.

After smoking for most of her life, Evelyn Gilson has finally quit. She feels that if more people know about the dangers of secondhand smoke, they will stop. Her decision comes too late to help her husband. However, there is still time to protect the health of others, especially children, who live with smokers.

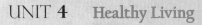

Fact-Finding Exercise

Read the passage once. Then read the following statements. Check whether they are True or False. If a statement is false, change the statement so that it is true. Then go back to the passage and find the line that supports your answer.

1. _____ True _____ False   Cigarette smoking causes many diseases.

                _____

2. _____ True _____ False   Evelyn Gilson has lung cancer.

                _____

3. _____ True _____ False   Secondhand smoke is the smoke from other people's cigarettes.

                _____

4. _____ True _____ False   People do not die from secondhand smoke.

                _____

5. _____ True _____ False   Children of smokers are sick more often than are children of nonsmokers.

                _____

6. _____ True _____ False   In the United States, you cannot smoke on any domestic airline flights.

                _____

PART 1

Skim through the passage. Then read the following statements. Choose the one that is the correct main idea of the reading.

a. Edward Gilson has lung cancer, but he has never smoked.

b. Secondhand smoke is very harmful to nonsmokers.

c. Nonsmokers often breathe in secondhand smoke.

Scan the passage. Work with a partner to fill in the flowchart below with information from the reading.

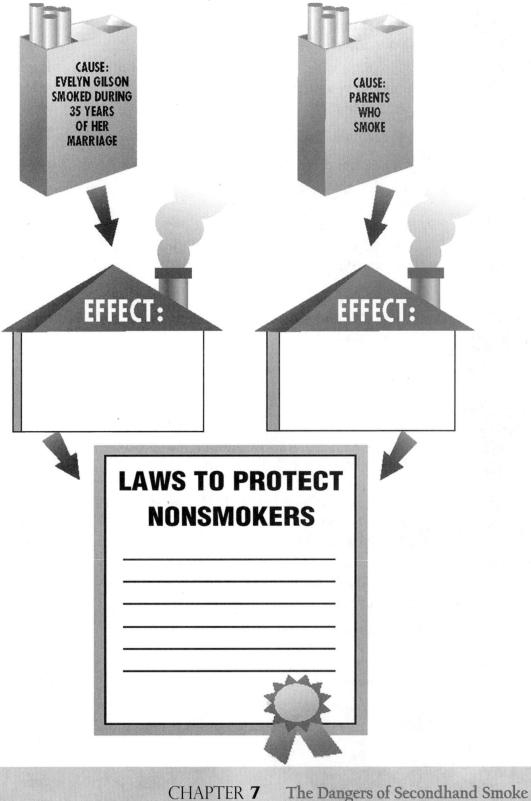

CAUSE:
EVELYN GILSON
SMOKED DURING
35 YEARS
OF HER
MARRIAGE

CAUSE:
PARENTS
WHO
SMOKE

EFFECT:

EFFECT:

LAWS TO PROTECT NONSMOKERS

Read each question carefully. Either circle the letter of the correct answer or write your answer in the space provided.

1. Scientific research shows that cigarette smoking causes many kinds of disease. **In fact,** many people who smoke get lung cancer.

   What kind of information follows **in fact?**

   a. more, specific information about the idea in the sentence before
   b. new, different information from the idea in the sentence before

2. No one knows **for sure** why Mr. Gilson has lung cancer. **Nevertheless,** doctors believe that secondhand smoke may cause lung cancer in people who do not smoke.

   a. **For sure** means
   1. definitely
   2. for example
   3. right now

   b. **Nevertheless** means
   1. in addition
   2. however
   3. in fact

3. Nonsmokers often breathe in the smoke from other people's cigarettes. This is secondhand smoke. Edward Gilson has been breathing **this type of smoke** for 35 years. Now he is dying of lung cancer. **However,** he is not alone. The **U.S. Environmental Protection Agency** reports that about 53,000 people die in the United States each year as a result of exposure to secondhand smoke.

   a. What is **this type of smoke?**

   _____

   b. **However** means
   1. but
   2. and
   3. so

c. **He is not alone.** This sentence means
1. his wife is also dying from lung cancer
2. he wife and family are with him
3. other nonsmokers are dying from lung cancer

d. Look at page 131. What is the **Environmental Protection Agency?**

_____

e. How do you know?

_____

f. This type of information is called a(n)
1. index
2. footnote
3. preface

4. In the past, scientists did not think that the chemicals in cigarette smoke could harm a nonsmoker's health. Recently, though, **scientists changed their opinion** after they studied a large group of nonsmokers.

What are scientists' opinions now?
a. Cigarette smoke can harm a nonsmoker's health.
b. Cigarette smoke cannot harm a nonsmoker's health.

5. The smoke that comes from a lit cigarette contains many different **poisonous** chemicals. Scientists discovered that even nonsmokers had unhealthy amounts of these toxic chemicals in their bodies. **As a matter of fact,** almost all of us breathe tobacco smoke at times.
a. In this paragraph, which word is a synonym of **poisonous?**

_____

b. What does **as a matter of fact** mean?
1. However
2. In fact
3. In addition

6. **Even though** many public places have nonsmoking areas, smoke flows in from the areas where smoking is permitted.
a. What does **even though** mean?
1. Because
2. As a result
3. Although

b. Read the following sentences. Write the words **even though** in the appropriate sentence.

1. Bob went to school _____ he was sick.

2. Bob went to the doctor's office _____ he was sick.

7. It is **even harder** for children to avoid secondhand smoke. This means

a. it is easier for adults to stay away from secondhand smoke.

b. it is easier for children to stay away from secondhand smoke.

8. In the United States, nine million children under the age of five live in homes with **at least** one smoker. Research shows that these children are sick more often than children who live in homes where no one smokes.
At least means

a. a minimum of

b. less than

c. more than

9. The children of smokers are **more than twice as likely** to develop lung cancer when they are adults as children of nonsmokers.

This sentence means that, compared to the children of nonsmokers,

a. children of smokers have double the chance of developing lung cancer

b. children of smokers will develop lung cancer more quickly

10. People are becoming very aware of the danger of secondhand smoke. **As a result,** they have passed laws that **prohibit** people from smoking in many public places. **Currently,** 45 states in the United States have laws that **restrict,** or limit, smoking. The most well-known law forbids people from smoking on **domestic** airline flights, **i.e.,** flights within the country.

a. **As a result** means

1. in addition

2. however

3. consequently

b. In this paragraph, which word is a synonym of **prohibit?**

_____

c. What does **currently** mean?
   1. Recently
   2. Right now
   3. In the future

d. What does **restrict** mean?

   _____

e. How do you know?

   _____

f. What information follows **i.e.?**
   1. An explanation
   2. A reason
   3. An example

g. What is a **domestic** flight?
   1. An airplane flight between cities in different countries
   2. An airplane flight between cities in the same country

D. *Think* About It

Read the following questions and think about the answers. Write your answer below each question. Then compare your answers with those of your classmates.

1. Edward Gilson developed lung cancer because he breathed secondhand smoke from his wife's cigarettes.

   a. How do you think he feels about this?

   _____

   b. How do you think Evelyn Gilson feels about this?

   _____

   c. What are some ways the Gilsons could have prevented Edward from getting lung cancer?

   _____

2. What are some ways of protecting children who live with parents who smoke?

   _____

E. DICTIONARY SKILLS

Read the dictionary entry for each word, and think about the context of the sentence. Write the number of the appropriate definition on the line next to the word. Then choose the sentence with the correct answer.

1.

> **avoid** *v.* **1** to stay away from, *(syn.)* to **bypass**: *She avoids walking on dark streets at night.* **2** to elude, evade: *The thief avoided capture by the police.* **3** to not do s.t., abstain from doing: *We avoid eating fattening foods.* -adj. **avoidable**; -adv. **avoidably.**

We cannot **avoid** secondhand smoke in restaurants and other public places. Even though many public places have nonsmoking areas, smoke flows in from the areas where smoking is permitted.

a. **avoid:** _____

b. 1. We cannot evade secondhand smoke in restaurants and other public places.

   2. We cannot stay away from secondhand smoke in restaurants and other public places.

   3. We cannot abstain from breathing secondhand smoke in restaurants and other public places.

2.

> **risk** *n.* **1** [C;U] a chance, danger of losing
> s.t. important: *When you buy land, you take*
> *the risk that it will lose value.* **2** [C] a
> person who may not do as good a job as one
> would like: *He is very smart, but he is a*
> *risk because he does not work very hard.*
> **3 at one's own risk:** agreeing that one is
> responsible for all problems or danger:
> *Swim at your own risk!* **4 run a risk:** to
> put oneself in danger: *If ask a question, do I*
> *run the risk of looking stupid?*

The children of smokers are more than twice as likely to develop lung cancer when they are adults as are children of nonsmokers. The **risk** of lung cancer is even higher for children who live in homes where both parents smoke.

a. **risk:** _____

b. 1. The person who does not do a good job of not smoking is more likely to get lung cancer if both parents smoke.

2. The chance of children getting lung cancer is higher for those children who live in homes where both parents smoke than where parents are nonsmokers.

3.

> **exposure** *n.* **1** [C;U] being unprotected,
> esp. from cold weather: *The lost mountain*
> *climbers suffered from exposure.* **2** [U] risk
> of loss: *We limit our exposure by investing*
> *only one quarter of the money.* **3** [C] a
> section of photographic film: *That roll of*
> *film contains 36 exposures.* **4** [C] a position
> or view in relation to a direction on the
> compass (north, south, east, or west): *The*
> *living room has a southern exposure.*

The U.S. Environmental Protection Agency reports that about 53,000 people die in the United States each year as a result of **exposure** to secondhand smoke.

a. **exposure:** _____

b. 1. About 53,000 people die in the United States each year as a result of being unprotected from secondhand smoke.

2. About 53,000 people die in the United States each year as a result of risking loss from secondhand smoke.

3. About 53,000 people die in the United States each year as a result of their position in relation to secondhand smoke.

Word Forms

PART 1

In English, the noun form and the verb form of some words are the same, for example, *cause (v.), cause (n.)*. Complete each sentence with the correct form of the words on the left. Then circle (*v.*) if you are using the verb, or (*n.*) if you are using a noun. **Write all of the verbs in the present tense. The verbs may be affirmative or negative. The nouns may be singular or plural.**

report

1. a. Mark writes several short _____ on public
   (v., n.)
   health every month.

   b. He usually _____ on nutrition and exercise.
   (v., n.)

damage

2. a. Direct exposure to the sun _____ the eyes.
   (v., n.)

   b. Consequently, never look directly into the sun in order to
   avoid any chance of eye _____.
   (v., n.)

limit

3. a. If smokers _____ their children's exposure to
   (v., n.)
   cigarette smoke, the children will have a much higher risk
   of becoming sick.

   b. Therefore, parents need to put a definite _____
   (v., n.)
   on the amount of smoking they do at home.

study

4. a. The EPA publishes all of its _____ when
   (v., n.)
   they are complete.

   b. The EPA _____ the quality of the air and
   (v., n.)
   water in the United States.

result
     5. a. Smoking cigarettes _____ in lung cancer
                         (v., n.)
          for every smoker.

        b. For example, Evelyn Gilson does not have lung cancer.
          However, the usual _____ of smoking are fre-
                              (v., n.)
          quent colds, and other diseases of the lungs.

PART 2

In English, some adjectives become nouns by adding the suffix -ness, for example, *quick (adj.), quickness* (n.). Complete each sentence with the correct form of the word on the left. **The nouns may be singular or plural.**

sick *(adj.)*
     1. a. Phil was quite _____ last month.
sickness *(n.)*
        b. Because his _____ was very severe, he stayed in
          bed for three weeks.

aware *(adj.)*
     2. a. Lisa wanted me to be _____ of the heavy traffic
awareness *(n.)*
          on the highway.
        b. My _____ of bad driving conditions saved me a
          lot of time.

near *(adj.)*
     3. a. The curious dog came very _____ the small child.
nearness *(n.)*
        b. The little girl was uncomfortable with the _____
          of such a big animal, and she began to cry.

late *(adj.)*
     4. a. The teacher has strict rules about being _____.
lateness *(n.)*
        b. In fact, if a student has several _____, she will not
          allow him in class anymore.

weak *(adj.)*
     5. a. Alice went to the doctor because she was feeling a
weakness *(n.)*
          _____ in her legs.
        b. The doctor told her that she felt _____ because
          she didn't exercise enough.

Another Look

Read the following information about smoking. Then answer the questions which follow.

Smoking Facts and Figures

Many people, including doctors, parents, teachers, and others, are concerned about the health risks of cigarette smoking. According to the latest statistics, active smoking kills 400,000 smokers in the United States each year, and secondhand smoke kills 53,000 nonsmokers in the United States each year. Equally disturbing is the fact that 80% of smokers have their first cigarette before they are 18 years old.

Before trying to solve the health problems related to cigarette smoking, an important question to ask is why people start smoking to begin with. Some factors involved in beginning to smoke are environmental. For example, family history influences whether or not a child becomes a smoker. When parents smoke, they model smoking behavior, and children often copy what they see their parents do. Many people, especially young people, have their first cigarette because of peer pressure. They want to be accepted in their social group, and if smoking is part of the group's activities, young people will begin to smoke in order to be accepted into the group.

Personal factors also affect whether a person will begin to smoke. People with tendencies toward risk-taking behavior are more likely to start smoking than people who tend not to take risks. Outgoing people are also more likely to become smokers than shy people are. People also take up smoking to alleviate stress, or to help themselves lose weight. Finally, people, especially young people, begin to smoke because they believe smoking makes them appear mature, self-confident, and independent.

When we understand the reasons why people become smokers, we can help smokers become nonsmokers again. We can also help nonsmokers remain lifetime nonsmokers.

QUESTIONS FOR ANOTHER LOOK

1. How many smokers die in the United States every year from smoking?
   a. 400,000
   b. 53,000

2. How many nonsmokers die in the United States every year from second-hand smoke?
   a. 400,000
   b. 53,000

3. How old are most smokers when they have their first cigarette?

   _____

4. What factors influence why people start smoking? Put a check mark next to the factors that are important.
   a. _____ Family history
   b. _____ Peer pressure
   c. _____ Money
   d. _____ Risk-taking behavior
   e. _____ Stress
   f. _____ Education

5. According to the article, why is it important to understand the reasons people start smoking?

   _____

1. Role Play: work with another student.

   Student 1: You are a nonsmoker. You are sitting in a restaurant. The person sitting at the table next to you is smoking. Politely ask that person to put out the cigarette.

   Student 2: You are a smoker. You are sitting in a restaurant smoking a cigarette. The person at the next table politely asks you to put out your cigarette. Respond to the person's request.

2. Work in small groups. Pretend that you are the lawmakers in your city, state, or country. Make up laws about smoking. Decide where people can smoke and where they cannot smoke. Present your laws to the class. Give reasons for your decisions.

3. Work in small groups. You represent smokers. You do not want new laws that prohibit smoking. Prepare reasons why you think prohibiting smoking is a bad idea.

4. Advertisements are designed to make people want to buy and use a particular product. Look through magazines and newspapers for a cigarette advertisement. Bring it to class. In groups, discuss the advertisement. Why might it make someone want to buy and smoke cigarettes? What do you think of these reasons?

5. Work in pairs or small groups. You are an advertiser for a tobacco company. Design an advertisement for your cigarette.

6. Work in pairs or small groups. You are on the Committee for Public Health. Design an advertisement to show the dangers of smoking.

I. Topics FOR Discussion AND Writing

1. Many people believe that people have a right to smoke wherever they want. Do you agree or disagree with this opinion? Explain your answer.

2. Many people believe that cigarettes should be illegal, just like marijuana or certain drugs. Do you agree or disagree with this opinion? Why?

3. Are there laws in your country about smoking? List them. Compare the laws in your country with the laws in your classmates' countries.

4. **Write in your journal.** Explain why you think it is or is not right for a government to tell people where they can or cannot smoke.

Word Search

Read the words listed below. Find them in the puzzle and circle them. They may be written in any direction.

avoid	danger	harmful	prohibit
awareness	develop	likely	restrict
chemical	disease	nevertheless	toxic
currently	exposure	nonsmoker	

```
L  L  J  S  I  W  N  R  N  U  E  N  H  Q  L
I  J  P  X  C  V  S  S  E  N  E  R  A  W  A
H  G  N  V  I  U  K  L  Q  V  I  X  R  B  L
E  A  O  P  X  P  R  W  E  O  T  Y  M  F  W
O  F  N  D  O  R  P  R  L  U  C  L  F  H  H
J  G  S  E  T  O  T  U  E  W  I  E  U  Q  D
R  F  M  V  Z  H  Q  U  X  N  R  K  L  A  G
C  Z  O  E  E  I  D  X  P  T  T  I  H  N  Y
P  G  K  L  S  B  S  I  O  Q  S  L  J  J  I
F  Y  E  O  U  I  T  V  S  X  E  Z  Y  Z  J
F  S  R  P  N  T  S  T  U  E  R  Y  I  F  T
S  M  E  D  A  N  G  E  R  D  A  V  O  I  D
Y  A  P  L  A  C  I  M  E  H  C  S  D  K  N
R  J  T  I  W  I  E  D  U  G  W  N  E  P  C
```

Read the clues on the next page. Write the answers in the correct spaces in the puzzle.

Crossword Puzzle Clues

Across Clues

1. Try to stay away from
4. Two times
5. 20 cigarettes in one box is a _____ of cigarettes.
6. The opposite of **bottom**
9. _____ smoke is the type of smoke you breathe in from someone else's cigarette.
12. Forbid; not allow
14. That is
15. Toxic
17. The opposite of **pull**
18. Cigarettes are made from this plant.
21. Schools, libraries, and restaurants are _____ places.
22. At the present time
23. The opposite of **come**

Down Clues

1. I _____ a student. You are a student.
2. This word refers to activities within a country.
3. Chance
7. A very serious disease
8. Dangerous
10. _____ though I studied, I did not pass the test.
11. Someone who does not smoke is a _____.
13. A disease of the lungs
16. The opposite of **sick**
19. Stop
20. When we breathe, air enters our _____.

Read the passage below. Complete each blank space with one of the prepositions listed below. You may use the prepositions more than once.

for	in	of	to

Most people know that cigarette smoking is harmful _____ (1) their health. Scientific research shows that it causes many kinds _____ (2) diseases. _____ (3) fact, many people who smoke get lung cancer. However, Edward Gilson has lung cancer, and he has never smoked cigarettes. He lives with his wife, Evelyn, who has smoked about a pack _____ (4) cigarettes a day throughout their marriage. The Gilsons have been married _____ (5) 35 years.

No one knows _____ (6) sure why Mr. Gilson has lung cancer. Nevertheless, doctors believe that secondhand smoke may cause lung cancer _____ (7) people who do not smoke. Nonsmokers often breathe _____ (8) the smoke from other people's cigarettes. This is second-hand smoke. Edward Gilson has been breathing this type _____ (9) smoke for 35 years. Now he is dying _____ (10) lung cancer. However, he is not alone. About 53,000 people die _____ (11) the United States each year as a result _____ (12) exposure _____ (13) second-hand smoke.

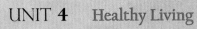

A Healthy Diet for Everyone

Prereading Preparation

1. Look at the photograph. Describe the two meals. Which meal do you think is healthier? Why?

2. Work with one or two partners. Fill in the chart below. What food do you think is healthy? What food is not?

3. Why is it important to have a healthy diet?

Food That Is Healthy	Food That Is Not Healthy

4. Read the title of this passage. People in different cultures and countries eat different kinds of food. What health food suggestions can you make that everyone around the world can follow? What does "A Healthy Diet for Everyone" mean?

A Healthy Diet for Everyone

1   Sometimes, people are confused about what type of food is healthy, and what kind of food can be harmful to our health. The USDA[1] has prepared a food guide to help people learn about which types of food are the healthiest to eat. The food guide describes six basic food groups: meat (beef, fish, chicken, etc.),
5   dairy (milk, yogurt, cheese, etc.), grains (bread, cereal, rice, etc.), fruit, and vegetables. The last group is fats, oil, and sweets. The USDA also suggests how much of each food group is healthy to eat daily. Although this guide was prepared by the U.S. government, it is very useful for people all over the world.

    As a result of years of research, we know that too much animal fat is bad for
10   our health. For example, Americans eat a lot of meat, and only a small amount of grains, fruit, and vegetables. Because of their diet, they have a high rate of cancer and heart disease. In Japan, in contrast, people eat large amounts of grains and very little meat. The Japanese also have a very low rate of cancer and heart disease. In fact, the Japanese live longer than anyone else in the world.
15   Unfortunately, when Japanese people move to the United States, the rate of heart disease and cancer increases as their diet changes. Moreover, as hamburgers, ice cream, and other high-fat foods become popular in Japan, the rate of heart disease and cancer is increasing there as well. People are also eating more meat and dairy products in other countries such as Cuba, Mauritius, and
20   Hungary. Not surprisingly, the disease rate in these countries is increasing along with the change in diet. Consequently, doctors everywhere advise people to eat more grains, fruit, and vegetables, and eat less meat and fewer dairy products.

    A healthy diet is important for children as well as adults. When adults have poor eating habits, their children usually do, too. After all, children eat the same
25   way as their parents. When parents eat healthy food, the children will learn to enjoy it, too. Then they will develop good eating habits. Doctors advise parents to give their children healthier snacks such as fruit, vegetables, and juice.

    Everyone wants to live a long, healthy life. We know that the food we eat affects us in different ways. For instance, doctors believe that fruit and
30   vegetables can actually prevent many different diseases. On the other hand, animal fat can cause disease. We can improve our diet now and enjoy many years of healthy living.

[1]The United States Department of Agriculture. The USDA's responsibility is to control the quality of food in the United States.

Fact-Finding Exercise

Read the passage once. Then read the following statements. Check whether they are True or False. If a statement is false, change the statement so that it is true. Then go back to the passage and find the line that supports your answer.

1. ____ True ____ False   There are six basic food groups.

   _____

2. ____ True ____ False   People can choose food from each group every day.

   _____

3. ____ True ____ False   Most Americans eat a lot of meat.

   _____

4. ____ True ____ False   Most Japanese eat very few grains.

   _____

5. _____ True _____ False   There is a high rate of cancer and heart disease in Japan.

_____

6. _____ True _____ False   Doctors think it is a good idea for people to eat less meat.

_____

7. _____ True _____ False   It is not important for children to have a healthy diet.

_____

8. _____ True _____ False   Children usually eat differently than their parents.

_____

9. _____ True _____ False   Doctors believe that fruit and vegetables cause different diseases.

_____

Skimming and Scanning Exercise

PART 1

Skim through the passage. Then read the following statements. Choose the one that is the correct main idea of the reading.

    a. The kind of diet we have can cause or prevent diseases.

    b. Doctors advise people to eat more fruit, vegetables, and grains.

    c. Eating meat causes cancer and heart disease.

Scan the passage. Work with a partner to fill in the flowchart below with information from the reading.

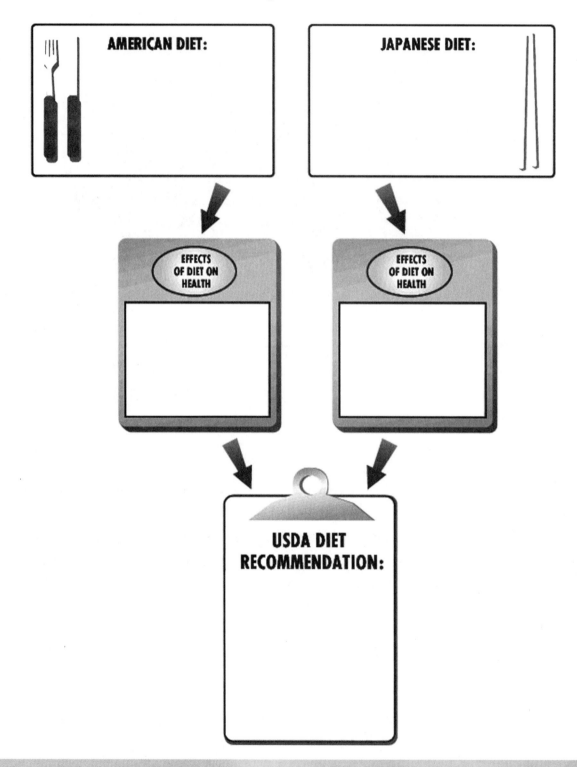

AMERICAN DIET:

JAPANESE DIET:

EFFECTS OF DIET ON HEALTH

EFFECTS OF DIET ON HEALTH

USDA DIET RECOMMENDATION:

Reading Analysis

Read each question carefully. Either circle the letter or the number of the correct answer or write your answer in the blank space.

1. Everyone knows that we must eat food **in order to** live.

   a. What information follows **in order to**?

      1. The reason
      2. The decision
      3. The cause

   b. Complete the following sentence with the appropriate choice.

      Cindy went to the supermarket in order to

      1. walk to the store
      2. learn how to cook
      3. buy some food

2. What type of food is healthy? What **kind** of food can be bad for our health?

   In these sentences, which word is a synonym for **kind**?

   _____

3. The **USDA** described **basic food groups:** meat (beef, fish, chicken, etc.), dairy (milk, cheese, butter, etc.), grains (bread, cereals, rice, etc.), fruit, vegetables, and a group including fats, oils, and sweets. The USDA suggested how much of each food group was healthy to eat **daily.**

   a. Refer to page 154. What is the **USDA**?

      _____

   b. How do you know?

      _____

   c. This information is called a

      _____

d. What are the basic food groups? Give examples of each group.

1. _____

2. _____

3. _____

4. _____

5. _____

6. _____

e. What does **daily** mean?
   1. Every day
   2. A lot of
   3. A little of

4. Americans eat a lot of meat, and only a small amount of grains, fruit, and vegetables. In Japan, **in contrast,** people eat large amounts of grains and very little meat. The Japanese also have a very low rate of cancer and heart disease. **In fact,** the Japanese live longer than **anyone else** in the world.

   a. What information follows **in contrast**?
      1. A similar idea
      2. An opposite idea
      3. The same idea

   b. What information follows **in fact**?
      1. More information about the same idea
      2. Contrasting information about the same idea
      3. Surprising information about the same idea

   c. What does **anyone else** mean?
      1. All other people
      2. Some other people
      3. Most other people

5. **Unfortunately,** when Japanese people move to the United States, the rate of heart disease and cancer increases **as** their diet changes. **Moreover,** as hamburgers, ice cream, and other high-fat foods become popular in Japan, the rate of heart disease and cancer increases **there,** too.

   a. What follows **unfortunately**?
      1. Something lucky
      2. Something bad
      3. Something false

   b. What does **as** mean?
      1. When
      2. So
      3. And

   c. What does **moreover** mean?
      1. However
      2. Also
      3. Then

   d. What are some examples of high-fat foods?

      _____

   e. Where does **there** refer to?
      1. In the United States
      2. In Cuba
      3. In Japan

6. People are also eating more meat and dairy products in other countries **such as** Cuba, Mauritius, and Hungary. **Not surprisingly,** the disease rate in these countries is increasing along with the change in diet. **Consequently,** doctors everywhere advise people to eat more grains, fruit, and vegetables, and less meat and fewer dairy products.

   a. What does **such as** mean?
      1. For example
      2. Instead of
      3. Except in

b. What information follows **not surprisingly**?
   1. Information that is hard to believe
   2. Information that is not true
   3. Information that is easy to believe

c. What does **consequently** mean?
   1. In addition
   2. As a result
   3. In fact

7. A healthy diet is important for children **as well as** adults.

   a. This sentence means that a healthy diet
      1. is more important for children than it is for adults
      2. is more important for adults than it is for children
      3. is equally important for both adults and children

   b. **As well as** means
      1. and also
      2. but not
      3. instead of

8. When adults have poor eating habits, their children usually do, too. **After all,** children eat the same way as their parents.

   a. The first sentence means
      1. the children usually have better eating habits
      2. the children also have poor eating habits

   b. Read the second sentence again. Then read the following sentence and complete it with the appropriate choice.
      José speaks Spanish fluently. After all,
      1. he lived in Venezuela for 15 years
      2. he reads many books about South America

9. Most doctors agree that fruit and vegetables can actually **prevent** many different diseases. **On the other hand,** animal fat can **cause** disease.

    a. What is the connection between **prevent** and **cause**?

        1. They have similar meanings.

        2. They have opposite meanings.

    b. What does **prevent** mean?

        1. To keep from happening

        2. To make happen

    c. What information follows **on the other hand**?

        1. A similar idea

        2. An example of the idea

        3. An opposite idea

    d. Read the following sentences. Complete the second sentence with the appropriate choice.

    I may visit many different places on my vacation. On the other hand,

        1. I may go to museums, zoos, parks, and beaches

        2. I may stay at home and relax

D. *Think* About It

Read the following questions and think about the answers. Write your answer below each question. Then, compare your answers with those of your classmates.

1. Why did the USDA prepare a food guide for Americans?

   _____

2. Why are fats, oils, and sweets grouped together?

   _____

3. Why do Japanese people change their diet when they move to the United States?

   _____

E. DICTIONARY SKILLS

Read the dictionary entry for each word, and think about the context of the sentence. Write the number of the appropriate definition on the line next to the word. Then choose the sentence with the correct answer.

1.
> **confuse** *v.* **-fused, -fusing, -fuses**
> **1** to mix things up: *He sent the wrong reports because he confused them with other ones.* **2** to mix up mentally so that one cannot understand or think clearly: *The teacher's question confused him.*

Sometimes, people are **confused** about what type of food is healthy and what kind of food can be bad for our health.

a. **confused:** _____

b. 1. Sometimes, people mix up healthy food and unhealthy food.

   2. Sometimes, people feel mixed up and cannot understand which kinds of food are healthy and which kinds are not.

2.

> **prevent** *v.* **1** to stop from happening, avoid: *He prevented an accident by braking his car just in time.* **2** to stop s.o. from doing s.t.: *The rain prevented me from going.*

Doctors believe that fruit and vegetables can actually **prevent** many different diseases.

a. **prevent:** _____

b. 1. Doctors believe that fruit and vegetables can help people avoid many different diseases.

   2. Doctors believe that fruit and vegetables can stop diseases from making people sick.

3.

> **suggest** *v.* **1** to propose s.t. to do or to offer an idea for consideration: *He suggested that we have lunch at the hotel.* **2** to bring (an idea) to mind, to indicate: *This picture suggests an ancient battle scene.* ‖ *The results of the test suggested that I was ill.*

The USDA **suggested** how much of each food group was healthy to eat daily.

a. **suggest:** _____

b. 1. The USDA brought to mind how much of each food group was healthy to eat daily.

   2. The USDA offered people an idea of how much of each food group was healthy to eat daily.

PART 1

In English, some verbs become nouns by adding the suffix -*ment,* for example, *announce (v.), announcement (n.).* Complete each sentence with the correct form of the words on the left. **Write all the verbs in the simple present tense. They may be affirmative or negative. The nouns may be singular or plural.**

improve *(v.)*
improvement *(n.)*

1. a. Manufacturers have made many _____ in computers in the last ten years. For example, they are smaller, faster, and more dependable.
   b. Manufacturers_____ their products to satisfy their customers.

agree *(v.)*
agreement *(n.)*

2. a. Some people are vegetarians. They think that eating meat is unhealthy. However, Faye _____ with the vegetarians.
   b. Faye believes that eating meat occasionally causes no health problems. However, she is in _____ with the idea that vegetables and fruit are very healthy.

encourage *(v.)*
encouragement *(n.)*

3. a. Jason is my best friend. He always_____ me when I have a difficult problem.
   b. In fact, his _____ has often helped me to succeed.

develop *(v.)*
development *(n.)*

4. a. Scientists are working to _____ a cure for all kinds of cancer.
   b. The _____ of a cure will be welcome all around the world.

enjoy *(v.)*
enjoyment *(n.)*

5. a. I _____ going to the movies alone. I prefer to go with a friend.
   b. Watching a movie with a friend adds to my _____.

In English, the noun form and the verb form of some words are the same, for example, *move (v.)*, *move (n.)*. Complete each sentence with the correct form of the word on the left. Circle *(v.)* if you are using a verb, or *(n.)* if you are using a noun. **Write all the verbs in the simple present tense. They may be affirmative or negative. The nouns may be singular or plural.**

research

1. a. Dr. Johnson _____ cures for cancer.
        (v., n.)

    b. She does all her _____ on heart disease.
        (v., n.)

increase

2. a. During the summer, the temperature _____
        about 30°.   *(v., n.)*

    b. This significant _____ in temperature usually
        (v., n.)
        makes many people uncomfortable.

taste

3. a. I like the sweet _____ of fruit such as cherries,
        (v., n.)
        pears, and peaches.

    b. Lemons _____ sweet, however. They are very sour.
        (v., n.)

cause

4. a. There are many _____ of cancer.
        (v., n.)

    b. For example, sometimes, exposure to the sun
        _____ skin cancer.
        (v., n.)

change

5. a. In some areas of the world, there are four _____
        in season: spring, summer, fall, and winter.   *(v., n.)*

    b. However, in other countries, the climate _____
        (v., n.)
        at all. It is the same all year. There is only one season.

Read the following passage about reasons why people eat when they're not hungry. Then answer the questions which follow.

Why Do I Eat When I'm Not Hungry?

The next time you want to eat something, ask yourself a question. Are you *really* hungry? If you answer "No," then ask yourself why you want to eat when your body is not really hungry. The following reasons may help you understand why you do so.

- I'M BORED. Sometimes we are bored and don't have anything better to do. When this happens, and you start to walk into the kitchen, stop yourself. Go to another part of the house, or go for a walk.

- IT TASTES GOOD. Sometimes it does, but sometimes we eat anything we can find in the kitchen, even if it really isn't that great tasting. When I'm dieting, I like to eat food that I *really* enjoy. Eat less of it, and enjoy it.

- I HAVE A LOT OF STRESS. This is often a common reason for eating. I often eat because of stress, not because I am hungry. I try to read a book, or exercise instead.

- TV MAKES ME WANT TO EAT. I rarely watched TV when I was thin. Then I started to watch TV almost every evening, and I gained 45 pounds. Evening TV programs have many food commercials that make me run to the kitchen for a snack. My best advice is to stop watching evening television.

- BECAUSE I'M REALLY THIRSTY. Sometimes people eat because they are thirsty. Instead of having something to drink, people eat something that is often fattening. The next time you feel hungry, drink some water.

If your stomach is making noise, it is time to eat. If you want food between meals when your stomach is *not* making noise, don't eat. Remember, you should give your body some kind of nutrition three times a day. If you do have to eat between meals, eat a piece of fruit or a vegetable. Try to think about what and why you are eating the next time you want a snack. Ask yourself, "Why am I eating?"

QUESTIONS FOR ANOTHER LOOK

1. What is the main idea of the story?
   a. There are many reasons why people eat when they are hungry.
   b. There are many reasons why people eat when they are not hungry.
   c. Watching television makes people eat when they are not hungry.

2. What are some reasons why people eat when they are not hungry?
   a. _____
   b. _____
   c. _____
   d. _____
   e. _____

3. Instead of eating when you are not hungry, what are some other things you can do?

   _____

   _____

1. The U.S. Department of Health and Human Services has prepared a Food Guide Pyramid to help people build a healthy diet for themselves. Read the suggested daily servings of each food group. Read the definitions of a serving for each food group.

   a. Use the Food Guide Pyramid and the serving descriptions to plan a one-day healthy diet. Write your diet in the chart on page 171. Then show your servings in the pyramid on page 172.

   b. Compare your one-day healthy diet with those of your classmates. In what ways are they similar? In what ways are they different?

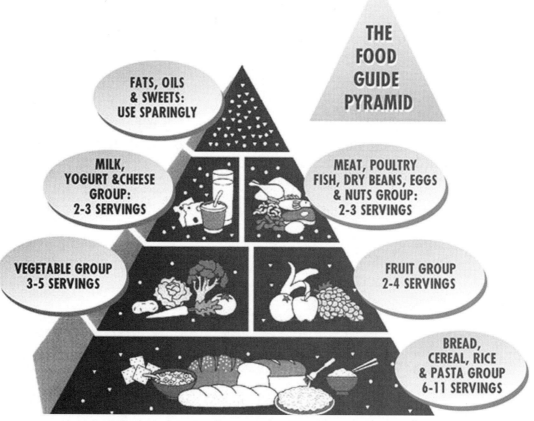

FOOD GUIDE PYRAMID

WHAT'S A SERVING?

milk, yogurt, and cheese (2–4 servings daily)
1 cup of milk
1 cup of yogurt
1½ ounces of cheese

vegetable group (3–5 servings daily)
6 oz. juice
½ cup cut-up vegetable
1 cup leafy green vegetable

fruit group (2–3 servings daily)
1 medium apple, banana, or orange
1 melon wedge
½ cup chopped fruit or berries
¼ cup dried fruit

meat, poultry, fish (2–4 servings daily)
2–3 ounces cooked meat, fish, or poultry

dry beans, eggs, and nuts group
(2–3 servings daily)
dry beans: ½ cup cooked dried peas or beans
1 egg
2 tablespoons seeds or nuts

bread, cereal, rice, and pasta group
(6–11 servings daily)
1 slice of bread
1 ounce of prepared (dry) cereal
½ cup cooked cereal
½ cup cooked rice
½ cup cooked pasta

A One-Day Health Diet					
Breakfast	(Snack)	Lunch	(Snack)	Dinner	(Snack)

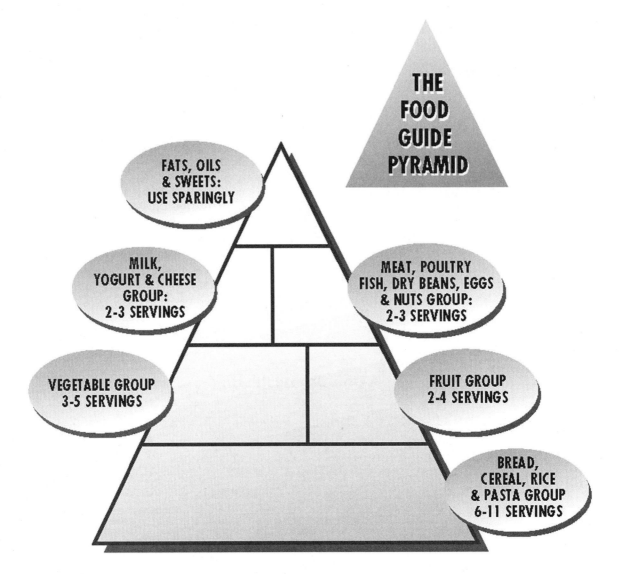

THE FOOD GUIDE PYRAMID

FATS, OILS & SWEETS: USE SPARINGLY

MILK, YOGURT & CHEESE GROUP: 2-3 SERVINGS

MEAT, POULTRY FISH, DRY BEANS, EGGS & NUTS GROUP: 2-3 SERVINGS

VEGETABLE GROUP 3-5 SERVINGS

FRUIT GROUP 2-4 SERVINGS

BREAD, CEREAL, RICE & PASTA GROUP 6-11 SERVINGS

2. Larry is a student at the state university. The following menu shows what he usually eats for breakfast, lunch, and dinner. What changes can you make to Larry's menu in order to make it healthier for him? Use the pyramid above to help you.

Breakfast:
two eggs
two slices of white bread with butter
one cup of coffee with cream and sugar

Lunch:
one large chocolate ice-cream cone

Dinner:
one hamburger on a roll
one large order of French fries
an order of broccoli
lettuce and tomatoes

Late-night snack:
a bag of potato chips
an apple

3. Alone, or with one or more classmates, go to a fast-food restaurant. Order a *healthy* meal. Report back to the class. Describe the meal you ate and explain why it was nutritious.

4. Alone, or with a student from your country, prepare a menu for a typical breakfast, lunch, and dinner in your country. Then talk to a student from another country and show the student your menu. Explain why you think your diet is healthy. Then ask the other student to explain why he or she thinks his/her diet is healthy. Compare your menu with the student's menu from a different country. Discuss which diet you both think is healthier.

I. Topics FOR *Discussion* AND *Writing*

1. Is there a high rate of heart disease and cancer in your country? What do you think are some reasons for this?

2. The reading passage discusses a healthy diet as a way to prevent disease. Work with a classmate. Make a list of other ways to prevent disease. Compare your list with those of your classmates.

3. Do you have children? What kind of food do you give them? Why? Do they enjoy the food? If you don't have children, imagine that you do. What kind of food do you give them? Why?

4. **Write in your journal.** Describe the ways you help yourself live a healthy life.

Read the words listed below. Find them in the puzzle and circle them. They may be written in any direction.

avoid	cholesterol	fruit	prevent
cancer	diet	healthy	recommend
children	fattening	parents	vegetables

```
O  C  V  Y  D  N  E  M  M  O  C  E  R  B  T
Y  T  H  R  Z  F  V  C  Y  H  T  L  A  E  H
C  H  I  L  D  R  E  N  O  N  Z  H  I  B  W
J  T  V  N  J  U  G  L  L  A  S  D  C  N  Y
P  V  F  A  T  T  E  N  I  N  G  Q  D  F  W
P  A  C  G  W  S  T  D  X  F  P  Z  E  W  M
X  L  R  A  T  H  A  I  X  R  C  Y  B  A  F
P  E  Y  E  N  P  B  O  E  U  K  E  Z  C  R
J  L  R  Q  N  C  L  V  O  I  G  M  R  E  Q
R  O  I  K  P  T  E  A  D  T  U  G  S  Z  G
L  C  N  I  D  N  S  R  P  Q  Z  X  M  V  M
Q  Z  V  K  T  G  T  X  E  T  V  M  W  J  S
```

Read the clues on the next page. Write the answers in the correct spaces in the puzzle.

Crossword Puzzle Clues

Across Clues

4. Study very carefully

5. As a result

7. The opposite of **yes**

9. The opposite of **on**

11. Also; furthermore

12. In good physical condition

13. Rice and cereals are _____ .

14. Keep from happening

17. The opposite of **down**

19. When we make many _____, we make things better.

20. The opposite of **no**

22. Illness; sickness

23. The opposite of **bottom**

Down Clues

1. I am. She _____.

2. Every day

3. Type

5. _____ is a very serious illness.

6. Unhappily

8. You have a choice: you can have either coffee _____ tea.

10. _____ and vegetables are very healthy for us to eat.

13. There are six basic food _____.

15. Milk, butter, and ice cream are _____ products.

16. I am _____ I don't understand what you said.

18. He is. We _____.

21. Chicken, pork, and beef are types of _____.

22. Everything we eat is part of our _____.

Grammar Cloze Quiz

a high rate of	fewer	too much
a lot of	large amounts of	very little
a small amount of	less	
a very low rate of	more	

Read the passage below. Complete each blank space with one of the words or phrases listed above. You may use them more than once. In addition, *there may be more than one correct answer.*

As a result of years of research, we know that _____ animal
(1)

fat is bad for our health. For example, Americans eat _____
(2)

meat, and _____ grains, fruit, and vegetables. Because of their
(3)

diet, they have _____ cancer and heart disease. In Japan, in con-
(4)

trast, people eat _____ grains and _____ meat. The
(5)   (6)

Japanese also have _____ cancer and heart disease. In fact, the
(7)

Japanese live longer than anyone else in the world. Consequently, doctors

everywhere advise people to eat _____ grains, fruit, and vegeta-
(8)

bles, and eat _____ meat and _____ dairy products.
(9)   (10)

There are many steps that we can take to help ourselves have a healthy life. With a classmate or in a small group, discuss what you can do to have a healthy life.

V I D E O   R E P O R T : Ten Healthy Foods

1. The video reports on ten types of food that help prevent diseases. Can you guess what they are?

2. Watch the video once or twice. Check whether the statements are true (T) or false (F). Correct the false answers with your classmates.

   a. ____ T ____ F   Tomatoes increase your risk of cancer.

   b. ____ T ____ F   There are many kinds of dairy food on the list.

   c. ____ T ____ F   One type of fatty fish that lowers cholesterol is salmon.

   d. ____ T ____ F   A small amount of green tea may damage people's health.

   e. ____ T ____ F   Broccoli is one of the best disease fighters, even though the first President Bush didn't like it.

   f. ____ T ____ F   Chocolate contains chemicals that help prevent heart disease.

3. Were you surprised that eggs were on the list of healthy foods? Which foods surprised you? How many of the ten foods do you eat every day?

Surfing THE *INTERNET*

Do an Internet search on one of the ten foods mentioned in the CNN report or some other food that you like. What health benefits does it have? Does it help prevent disease? Can it damage health?

Optional Activity: Ask your family doctor which web sites he or she can recommend. Share this information with your class. Find some Web sites on the Internet by looking up the key word "health" or "nutrition."

UNIT 5

INTERNATIONAL
SCIENTISTS

Alfred Nobel: A Man of Peace

Prereading Preparation

1. Look at the photograph on the left. This medal is a Nobel Prize. Alfred Nobel's image is in the center of the medal. What are the reasons why Alfred Nobel is famous?

   a. He established the Nobel Prize.

   b. He lived in the nineteenth century.

   c. He invented dynamite.

   d. He was Swedish.

2. What do you know about Alfred Nobel? Work with a partner. Make a list of the facts you know about Alfred Nobel.

   _____

   _____

3. Read the title of this passage. Why do you think Alfred Nobel is called a man of peace?

   _____

   _____

Alfred Nobel: A Man of Peace

1 The headline in the newspaper announced the death of Alfred Nobel on April 13, 1888. The reporter called him a salesman of death, "The Dynamite King," because he invented this powerful explosive. In fact, Alfred Nobel's dynamite business had made him a very rich man. The newspaper story

5 continued, giving Alfred Nobel's age, nationality, and other information about his business. However, the words "The Dynamite King" were all that the 55-year-old Swedish man read.

Alfred Nobel sadly put down the newspaper. No, he wasn't dead—his brother Ludwig had died the day before, and the French newspaper had made a

10 mistake. All the same, Alfred Nobel was disturbed. Was this the way the world was going to remember him? He did not like that idea at all. He had spent his life working for peace in the world. He hated violence and war. He had invented dynamite to *save* lives—lives that were lost because other explosives were dangerous to use. He wanted people to remember him as a man of peace.

15 Alfred Nobel invented dynamite at a perfect moment in time. Many countries were beginning to build railroads and tunnels, and needed a safe, powerful explosive to construct railroad tracks through mountains. People also needed dynamite to blow up stone in order to construct buildings, dams, and roads. Alfred Nobel invented dynamite for these peaceful uses. Moreover, he believed that

20 if all countries had the same powerful weapons, they would see how impossible war was, and wars would end. In fact, this was a popular idea of his day.

Nobel was very upset about the image that the world had of him, but he did not know what to do about it. He thought about his problem for years. He wanted to think of the best way for people to use his fortune of $9 million after

25 his death. Then, in 1895, an adventurer named Salomon August Andree made plans for an expedition to reach the North Pole. People all over the world were excited about Andree's journey. Nobel read about Andree's plan, too, and had an inspiration. He finally knew what to do with his fortune. He wrote his Last Will and Testament[1]. In his will, he instructed people to use all of his money for an

30 annual award to honor leaders of science, literature, and world peace. He stated that these leaders could be men or women of any nationality.

Alfred Nobel died on December 10, 1896, at the age of 63. He was unmarried and had no children. People all over the world wondered who was going to get Nobel's money. They were amazed when they learned of Alfred Nobel's plan to

35 award annual prizes in the fields of physics, chemistry, medicine, literature, and peace. The first Nobel Prizes were awarded in 1901, and they very soon became the greatest honor that a person could receive in these fields. In 1969, an award for Economics was added.

[1]Last Will and Testament: A legal paper that states how a person wishes his or her possessions to be distributed after his or her death.

40 The report of Alfred Nobel's death had been a mistake, but the decision that he made because of this error gave the world the image he wanted. Alfred Nobel established the Nobel Prize, and the world thinks of him the way he wanted to be remembered: Alfred Nobel, man of peace.

Fact-Finding Exercise

Read the passage once. Then read the following statements. Check whether they are True or False. If a statement is false, change the statement so that it is true. Then go back to the passage and find the line that supports your answer.

1. _____ True _____ False   Alfred Nobel wanted people to remember him as "The Dynamite King."

_____

2. _____ True _____ False   Alfred Nobel died in 1888.

_____

3. _____ True _____ False   Alfred Nobel invented dynamite.

_____

4. _____ True _____ False   Alfred Nobel hated violence.

_____

5. _____ True _____ False   Only men can receive a Nobel Prize.

_____

6. _____ True _____ False   In 1895, Salomon August Andree received the first Nobel Prize.

_____

B. Skimming and Scanning Exercise

PART 1

Skim through the passage. Then read the following statements. Choose the one that is the correct main idea of the reading.

a. Alfred Nobel wrote his will after Andree went to the North Pole.

b. The Nobel Prize is an internationally famous award.

c. Alfred Nobel was a peaceful man who gave the world a great prize.

PART 2

Scan the passage. Work with a partner to fill in the chart below with information from the reading.

Alfred Nobel		
Accomplishment	**Reason**	**Result**
He invented dynamite.		
He established the Nobel Prize.		

Read each question carefully. Either circle the letter of the correct answer or write your answer in the space provided.

1. The newspaper story gave Alfred Nobel's age, nationality, and other information about his business. **However,** the words "The Dynamite King" were **all** that the 55-year-old Swedish man read.

   a. What does **however** mean?
      1. And
      2. But
      3. Then

   b. Complete the following sentence with the appropriate choice.
      Robert wanted to go to the beach. However,
      1. it rained, so he stayed home.
      2. he asked his friends to go with him.
      3. he brought his lunch and a big umbrella.

   c. What does "the words 'The Dynamite King' were **all** he read" mean?
      1. He read everything.
      2. These three words were the only words he read.
      3. He read these words completely.

2. The French newspaper made a mistake about Nobel. Ludwig Nobel died, not Alfred Nobel. **All the same,** Alfred Nobel was disturbed.
   What do these sentences mean?

   a. Because the news was a mistake, Alfred was not upset anymore.

   b. It did not matter that the news was a mistake. Alfred was still upset.

3. The world was going to remember him as "The Dynamite King." Alfred Nobel did not like that idea **at all.**

   This sentence means that

   a. he liked the idea a little

   b. he liked the idea a lot

   c. he did not like anything about the idea

4. Nobel invented dynamite to save lives—lives that were lost because other explosives were dangerous to use.

   What follows the dash (—)?

   a. A contrast

   b. An example

   c. An explanation

5. Alfred Nobel invented dynamite for peaceful uses. **Moreover,** he believed that if all countries had the same powerful weapons, they would see how impossible war was, and wars would end. This was a popular idea of **his day.**

   a. **Moreover** means

      1. however

      2. in addition

      3. as a result

   b. Complete the following sentence with the correct choice.

      Robert needed to learn English because he wanted to go to college in the United States. Moreover,

      1. he had to speak English to get a good job

      2. he hated to study and was a poor student

   c. **His day** refers to

      1. the day Nobel invented dynamite

      2. the year 1895

      3. the time that he lived

6. Nobel wanted to think of the best way for people to use his **fortune** of $9 million after his death.

   What is a synonym of **fortune?**

   a. Idea

   b. Plan

   c. Wealth

7. In 1895, Alfred Nobel wrote his **Last Will and Testament.** In his will, he instructed people to use all his money for an annual award.

   a. Look at page 181. What is a **Last Will and Testament?**

   _____

   b. How do you know?

   _____

   c. This information is called a

   _____

8. Alfred Nobel had a plan to award annual prizes in the **fields** of physics, chemistry, medicine, literature, and peace.

   a. What does **fields** mean?

   1. Occupation; job

   2. Subject; area

   3. Outdoor area

   b. Give some examples of **fields.**

   _____

9. The report of Alfred Nobel's death was a **mistake,** but the decision that he made because of this error gave the world the image he wanted.

   In this sentence, which word is a synonym of **mistake?**

   _____

D. *Think* About It

Read the following questions and think about the answers. Write your answers below each question. Then, compare your answers with those of your classmates.

1. Alfred Nobel invented dynamite to help people build railroads, tunnels, building, and dams, but the reporter in the story called Nobel "a salesman of death." Why?

   _____

2. How did Nobel earn his fortune of $9 million?

   _____

3. Nobel established the Nobel Prize so that people would remember him as a man of peace. Can you think of another reason why he wanted to give prizes to people who were leaders in their fields?

   _____

E. DICTIONARY SKILLS

Read the dictionary entry for each word and think about the context of the sentence. Write the number of the appropriate definition on the line next to the word. In addition, circle *noun, verb,* or *adjective* where indicated. Then choose the sentence with the correct answer.

1.

> **perfect** *adj.* **1** the best possible: *a perfect score* (or) *record* ‖ *If only the world were perfect!* **2** complete and faultless, with nothing wrong or missing: *This car is in perfect condition.* **3** appropriate and satisfactory in every respect: *The holiday decorations were perfect.* **4** total, complete, thorough: *a perfect fool* ‖ *a perfect stranger* -*v.* to make perfect, flawless, excellent: *She perfected her style of playing the piano by practicing eight hours a day.* -*n.* (in grammar) a verb tense that shows action completed at a certain time: *In the sentence, "I had finished my dinner when she phoned," the verb "had finished" is in the past perfect.*

Alfred Nobel invented dynamite at a **perfect** moment in time. Many countries were beginning to build railroads and tunnels and needed a safe, powerful explosive to construct railroad tracks through mountains.

a. **perfect:** _____ (adjective / verb / noun)

b. 1. Nobel invented dynamite at a satisfactory moment in time.

   2. Nobel invented dynamite at a complete and faultless moment in time.

   3. Nobel invented dynamite at the best possible moment in time.

2.

> **disturb** *v.* **1** to interrupt: *Bad dreams disturbed her sleep.* **2** to worry, upset: *The bad news disturbed him.*

The newspaper article that described Alfred Nobel as "The Dynamite King" **disturbed** him. Nobel did not want the world to remember him that way. He hated violence and war.

a. **disturb:** _____

b. 1. The newspaper article that described Alfred Nobel as "The Dynamite King" upset him.

   2. The newspaper article that described Alfred Nobel as "The Dynamite King" interrupted him.

3.

> **award** *v.* **1** to give a prize (honor, praise, etc.) to s.o.: *The school principal awarded a prize in history to the best student.* **2** to give, grant: *A buyer awarded a contract to the supplier.* *-n.* **1** a prize (honor, praise, etc.) given to s.o. for outstanding performance: *The teacher gave her best student an award.*

In his will, Alfred Nobel instructed people to use all of his money for an annual **award** to honor leaders of science, literature, and world peace.

a. **award:** _____ (noun / verb)

b. 1. Alfred Nobel instructed people to use all of his money for an annual grant to honor leaders of science, literature, and world peace.

   2. Alfred Nobel instructed people to use all of his money for an annual prize to honor leaders of science, literature, and world peace.

4.

> **honor** *n.* **1** [U] one's good reputation (for honesty, integrity, etc.): *He is a man of honor and is totally trustworthy.* **2** [C;U] praise, recognition from others: *She has the honor of being given an award.* **3** *sing.* privilege, distinction: *The mayor has the honor of introducing the President to the audience.* **4** [U] a term of address for a mayor or a judge: *His Honor the Mayor attended the meeting.* **5 on one's honor:** an agreement to do s.t. based on one's word, integrity: *You may take the examination without supervision, and you are on your honor not to cheat.* **6 with honors:** with high academic marks: *He graduated with honors. -v.* **1** to praise, give recognition to: *She was honored by the mayor with a good citizenship award.* **2** to show respect, *(syn.)* to **venerate**: *The son honors his parents by caring for them.* **3** to fulfill to a promise or obligation: *She honored her student loans by paying them.*

In his will, Alfred Nobel instructed people to use all of his money for an annual award to **honor** leaders of science, literature, and world peace.

a. **honor:** _____ (noun / verb)

b. 1. In his will, Alfred Nobel instructed people to use all of his money for an annual award to fulfill his obligation to leaders of science, literature, and world peace.

2. In his will, Alfred Nobel instructed people to use all of his money for an annual award to give recognition to leaders of science, literature, and world peace.

3. In his will, Alfred Nobel instructed people to use all of his money for an annual award to show respect to leaders of science, literature, and world peace.

PART 1

In English, some verbs become nouns by adding the suffix *-ion* or *-ation*, for example, *suggest (v.), suggestion (n.)*. Be careful of spelling changes, for example, *combine (v.), combination (n.)*. Complete each sentence with the correct form of the words on the left. **Write all the verbs in the simple past tense. They may be affirmative or negative. The nouns may be singular or plural.**

instruct *(v.)*
instruction *(n.)*

1. a. The teacher _____ the students to write their compositions in pen, to skip a line, and to put their names on their papers.
    b. The students followed her _____ carefully.

invent *(v.)*
invention *(n.)*

2. a. Thomas Edison, an American, _____ more than 1,000 useful items.
    b. His _____ include the light bulb, sound movies, and the phonograph, or record player.

construct *(v.)*
construction *(n.)*

3. a. The company finished the _____ of their new office building.
    b. The company _____ the building of steel. They built it with bricks and wood instead.

inspire *(v.)*
inspiration *(n.)*

4. a. When the general gave a speech to his soldiers, he _____ them to action.
    b. As a result of the general's _____ , the soldiers won the difficult battle.

continue *(v.)*
continuation *(n.)*

5. a. When Jenny graduated from high school, she _____ her education immediately.
    b. She went to college several years later. The _____ of her education had to wait until she saved enough money to pay her tuition.

PART 2

In English, there are several ways that verbs change to nouns. Some verbs become nouns by adding the suffix *-ment,* for example, *improve (v.), improvement (n.).* Complete each sentence with the correct form of the words on the left. **Write all the verbs in the simple past tense. They may be affirmative or negative. The nouns may be singular or plural.**

announce *(v.)*
announcement *(n.)*

1. a. Carol and Simon _____ their engagement yesterday. They plan to get married in two months.
    b. Their happy _____ surprised their friends.

excite *(v.)*
excitement *(n.)*

2. a. Lloyd went to a baseball game yesterday, but the game _____ him at all. He prefers to watch soccer games.
    b. However, I enjoy watching baseball games. I think there is a lot of _____ in a baseball game.

amaze *(v.)*
amazement (n.)

3. a. The magician was very talented, and he _____ the children with his wonderful tricks.
    b. He smiled at their look of _____ when he sawed a woman in half.

establish *(v.)*
establishment *(n.)*

4. a. The Board of Directors discussed the formal_____ of a law school at the university ten years ago.
    b. However, they _____ the law school until this year.

state *(v.)*
statement *(n.)*

5. a. The Governor made a few _____ last night.
    b. In his speech, he _____ that he planned to run for reelection next year and that he also planned to cut taxes.

ALFRED NOBEL.
Född d. 21 okt. 1833. Död d. 10 dec. 1896.
Nobelstiftelsens grundläggare.

Read the following description of how Nobel Prize winners are chosen. Then answer the questions which follow.

Choosing Nobel Prize Winners

Alfred Nobel gave more than $9 million of his fortune to establish annual Nobel Prizes. According to Nobel's instructions, the money is given to people who help humankind in some outstanding way in five fields: physics, chemistry, physiology (or medicine), literature, and peace. In addition to the cash prize, each Nobel Prize winner receives a gold medal.

The Nobel Foundation is the legal owner of the prize funds, but it does not award the prizes. The Foundation follows a list of Alfred Nobel's rules. One of the rules states that not all the prizes must be given out each year. In fact, no Nobel prizes were given for the years 1940–42.

Different groups give out each award. The Royal Swedish Academy of Sciences makes the physics and chemistry awards. The Karolinska Institute of Stockholm, Sweden, awards the physiology or medicine prize. The Nobel Prize for literature is awarded by the Swedish Academy. The Norwegian parliament chooses a committee of five people to award the Nobel Peace Prize. In 1969, a sixth prize was established in economics. The Royal Swedish Academy of Sciences makes this award, too.

Each of these institutions must receive the names of candidates before February 1 of each year. A jury of 12 people decide on a final candidate by majority vote. If there is no majority vote for any one candidate, the prize is not offered that year. The jury reviews the candidates and asks them many questions, including the following:

- Did you make the outstanding contribution in the previous year?

- Was your contribution the result of many years of research?

- Did you work with one, two, or three scientists as a team? (The prize may be divided.)

- Did your discovery depend on the work of another candidate? (Again, the prize may be divided.)

The first Nobel prizes were awarded on December 10, 1901, the fifth anniversary of Alfred Nobel's death. The amount of each prize was more than $40,000 at that time. Today each prize is more than $1 million.

QUESTIONS FOR ANOTHER LOOK

1. _____ True _____ False   Each prize must be given out every year.

2. Why do you think no prizes were given out from 1940 to 1942?

   _____

3. What happens if the jury of 12 people cannot agree on one candidate?

   _____

4. Read the following interview question again. "Did you make the outstanding contribution in the previous year?" Why do you think this information is important?

   _____

1. Work in groups of three or four. You are part of a committee that has to decide on a new category for the Nobel Prize. Remember, the fields now are physics, chemistry, medicine/physiology, literature, peace, and economics. Discuss the reasons why you think this seventh prize is a good idea. Compare your ideas with those of your classmates, then take a vote to decide on the new category.

2. Work in groups of three or four. You are part of a committee that has to decide to eliminate one category from the Nobel Prize awards. Discuss the reasons you think this prize is no longer necessary or desirable. Compare your reasons with those of the class. Take a vote to decide on which category to eliminate.

3. Go to the library. Ask the librarian for a book that contains a list of all the Nobel Prize winners (the Almanac). Make a list of the Nobel Prize winners from your country and/or another country you are interested in. Write down the year the people received their prize, and the field they received the prize in. Then choose one person and write about his or her achievement.

I. Topics FOR Discussion AND Writing

1. Pretend that you are wealthy. What do you want to happen to your property and money after you die? Write instructions.

2. Nominate a famous person for a Nobel prize in one of the six categories. Describe the person and explain why you believe he or she deserves a Nobel prize in that field.

3. Go to the library. Use an almanac to find the list of all the Nobel Prize winners. Select a Nobel Prize winner from any country in any field. Write about that man or woman, and why you think this person deserved the award.

4. Write a short biography of one of the Nobel Prize winners who interests you.

5. **Write in your journal.** Describe how you want people to remember you. Explain why you want people to remember you this way.

Word Search

Read the words listed below. Find them in the puzzle and circle them. They may be written in any direction.

annual	dangerous	honor	peaceful
award	explosives	information	powerful
construct	headlines	leader	remember

```
U  P  C  B  Q  O  J  G  S  Z  I  N  P  E  R
G  R  E  B  M  E  M  E  R  N  E  X  O  Q  Q
X  Q  T  R  I  G  N  I  F  W  K  V  W  U  X
K  M  S  E  V  I  S  O  L  P  X  E  E  K  Y
M  S  T  U  L  R  R  B  A  N  M  H  R  P  Y
S  X  C  D  O  M  P  T  U  N  I  L  F  M  R
F  H  A  N  A  R  G  A  V  R  N  V  U  F  L
S  E  O  T  P  P  E  A  C  E  F  U  L  E  L
H  H  I  Z  D  J  Q  G  L  M  P  H  A  V  F
N  O  T  C  U  R  T  S  N  O  C  D  H  L  E
N  U  O  K  M  C  A  P  M  A  E  S  L  R  F
S  T  F  J  C  S  N  W  B  R  D  M  K  H  S
O  K  Y  L  K  S  O  C  A  X  F  I  D  D  Q
```

Crossword Puzzle

Read the clues on the next page. Write the answers in the correct spaces in the puzzle.

Crossword Puzzle Clues

Across Clues

1. You and I

2. I spoke to John yesterday. _____ mother is visiting him.

4. Alfred Nobel's _____ was Swedish.

5. I don't want people to forget me. I want them to _____ me.

7. Laura and I like _____ class.

9. _____ is the explosive that made Nobel rich.

11. Bombs, guns, and tanks are powerful _____.

12. Bombs are _____. They blow up when they hit something.

16. The Nobel Prize is an _____ for a person's achievements.

17. Nobel hated fighting and war. He hated all kinds of _____.

19. Nine million dollars is a lot of money. To some people it is a _____.

21. Error

Down Clues

1. A _____ states how a person wishes his or her possessions to be distributed after death.

2. A _____ is the title of a newspaper article.

3. Alfred Nobel wanted to _____, to create, an explosive that was safe to use.

6. I have _____ pen. Do you have your pen?

8. Disturbed

9. Unsafe

10. Chemistry is a _____ of study.

13. The opposite of **war**

14. Certain

15. Build

18. **I, you, _____, she, it**

20. I called Sam on the phone. I spoke to _____ for a short time.

be	have	make	think
become	know	read	write

Read the passage below. Complete each blank space with the simple past tense of one of the verbs listed above. You may use the verbs more than once.

After Nobel _____ the newspaper story, he
(1)

_____ very upset about the image that the world
(2)

_____ of him. He _____ about his problem for
(3)   (4)

years. Then, in 1895, an adventurer names Salomon August Andree

_____ plans to reach the North Pole. People all over the world
(5)

_____ excited about Andree's journey. Nobel _____
(6)   (7)

about Andree's plan, too, and _____ an inspiration. He finally
(8)

_____ what to do with his fortune, and he _____ his
(9)   (10)

Last Will and Testament to give instructions for his plan.

Alfred Nobel died on December 10, 1896. He _____
(11)

unmarried, and _____ no children. People all over the world
(12)

_____ amazed when they _____ in the newspapers
(13)   (14)

about Alfred Nobel's plan. However, after his death, the Nobel Prize

_____ the greatest honor a person could achieve.
(15)

Marie Curie: A Twentieth-Century Woman

Prereading Preparation

1. Look at the photograph. This woman was Marie Curie.

   a. What was Marie Curie's profession?
      1. She was doctor.
      2. She was a scientist.
      3. She was an inventor.
   b. What kind of work did Marie Curie do?
      1. She helped sick people.
      2. She invented new chemicals.
      3. She did research.
   c. Where did Marie Curie do most of her work?
      1. in a laboratory
      2. in a hospital
      3. in an office

2. When did Marie Curie do most of her work?
   a. in the nineteenth century
   b. in the late nineteenth century and the early twentieth century
   c. in the twentieth century

3. Read the title of this passage. Marie Curie was born in 1867, but she is called a twentieth-century woman. What does this title mean?
   a. She lived and worked in the twentieth century.
   b. She died in the twentieth century.
   c. She was a modern-thinking person.

Marie Curie: A Twentieth-Century Woman

1   Marya Sklodowska was born on November 7, 1867, in Poland. Marya's father wanted his five children to become well educated. Unfortunately, the family was poor. In fact, Marya worked for six years to support her older sister Bronya so Bronya could study medicine at the Sorbonne in Paris. When Bronya
5   finished medical school in 1891, 23-year-old Marya Sklodowska went to Paris to begin her own education.

     Once she arrived in Paris, Marya changed her name to the French form, Marie. After living with Bronya and her husband for a short time, she moved to an inexpensive apartment near the university so she could study without
10   interruption. Marie's student life was extremely poor, but in spite of her difficult living conditions, she was happy.

     In July 1893, Marie passed her physics examination, first in her class. At this time, she met Pierre Curie, a young scientist. Marie and Pierre discovered that they had much in common. They both believed that science was the most
15   important part of their lives. They didn't care about money or about being comfortable. They fell in love, and were married on July 26, 1895. Marie and Pierre Curie were very happy. They discussed their work and the latest scientific events, such as the discovery of X rays.[1] Marie was interested in this research, and began to look for unknown elements that had such rays. Pierre Curie
20   stopped his own research in order to help Marie in her work. He realized that she was about to make an important discovery.

     In 1898, the Curies found two new elements that give off radiation. They named these elements polonium and radium. In those days, no one knew that such radioactive materials were dangerous. In fact, Marie Curie created the
25   word *radioactive* to describe these materials. They did not know that exposure to this radioactivity caused their constant fatigue and illnesses, and they kept working. Finally, in 1902, they proved the existence of radium.

     On June 25, 1903, Marie became the first woman to receive a doctor of science degree from the Sorbonne. Then she received an even greater award. In
30   1903, the Academy of Science at Stockholm, Sweden awarded the Nobel Prize in

---

[1] X rays: An invisible, high-energy form of light that can pass through many solid objects, such as the human body.

Physics to Marie and Pierre Curie and Henri Becquerel for their discoveries in radioactivity.

The Curies continued to work closely together until a tragic event occurred. On a rainy day in April, 1906, Pierre was killed in a street accident. Marie was heartbroken, but she continued working. Then, in 1910, she isolated radium. It was the biggest accomplishment of Marie Curie's career. In 1911, she received the Nobel Prize again, in Chemistry. She was the first woman to receive the Nobel Prize and the first person to receive it a second time.

Over the years, Marie's constant exposure to radiation continued to destroy her health. She died on July 4, 1934, from an illness caused by her life's work: radium. Marie Curie never cared about making any money from her discoveries. Her life had been one of hard work, perseverance, and self-sacrifice. However, in her personal life, she was happily married and had two daughters. Professionally, she made important discoveries and achieved greatness in her field.

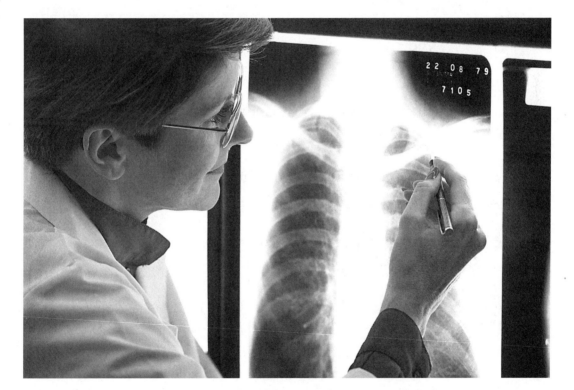

Fact-Finding Exercise

Read the passage once. Then read the following statements. Check whether they are True or False. If a statement is false, change the statement so that it is true. Then go back to the passage and find the line that supports your answer.

1. _____ True _____ False   Marie Curie was Marya Sklodowska.

_____

2. _____ True _____ False   Marie Curie was born in Paris.

_____

3. _____ True _____ False   Marie went to the university of Poland.

_____

4. _____ True _____ False   Marie's husband, Pierre, was a scientist.

_____

5. _____ True _____ False   The Curies discovered two new elements.

_____

6. _____ True _____ False   Radium made the Curies feel tired and sick.

_____

7. _____ True _____ False   Marie Curie was the first person to receive the Nobel Prize.

_____

8. _____ True _____ False   Marie Curie won the Nobel Prize twice.

_____

9. _____ True _____ False   Marie Curie wanted to earn a lot of money.

_____

Skimming and Scanning Exercise

PART 1

Skim through the passage. Then read the following statements. Choose the one that is the correct main idea of the reading.

a. Marie Curie discovered two new elements, polonium and radium.

b. Marie Curie was a great scientist who won the Nobel Prize twice.

c. Marie Curie did research on radioactive materials for many years.

PART 2

Scan the passage. Work with a partner. Look at the time line below for Marie Curie's life. Choose ten important dates in her life. Then, fill in the time line with the years you have chosen. On the lines below, write a sentence to describe what important event happened for each date.

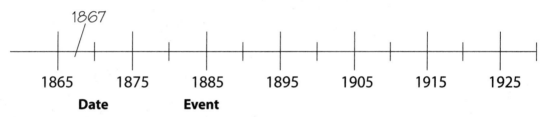

Date   **Event**

Example: 1867—Marie Curie is born.

1. _____

2. _____

3. _____

4. _____

5. _____

6. _____

7. _____

8. _____

9. _____

10. _____

Read each question carefully. Either circle the letter of the correct answer or write your answer in the space provided.

1. Marya's father wanted his five children to become well educated. **Unfortunately,** the family was poor.

   a. How many brothers and sisters did Marya have? _____

   b. This sentence means that
      1. none of the children went to a university
      2. all the children went to a university
      3. the family could not afford to send the children to a university

   c. Complete the following sentence with the correct choice.
      Marie and Pierre Curie worked well together for many years.
      Unfortunately,
      1. Pierre died when he was still young
      2. Pierre and Marie discovered two new elements
      3. Pierre and Marie shared the Nobel Prize in 1903

2. The family was poor. **In fact,** Marya **supported** her older sister Bronya until she finished medical school at the **Sorbonne** in Paris.

   a. This sentence means that
      1. Marya lived with her sister
      2. Marya gave her sister money to live on
      3. Marya helped her sister study

   b. What information follows **in fact?**
      1. Additional information that gives more details about the previous sentence
      2. Different information that introduces a new idea

   c. The **Sorbonne** is
      1. a business
      2. a hospital
      3. a school

3. **Once** she arrived in Paris, Marya changed her name to the French form, Marie.

   In this context, **once** means

   a. one time

   b. when

   c. before

4. Marya's student life was very poor, but **in spite of** her **difficult living conditions,** she was happy.

   a. This sentence means that

      1. Marya's living conditions made her happy because they were difficult

      2. Marya's living conditions were bad, but she was happy

   b. Read the following sentences. Write **in spite of** in the appropriate sentence.

      1. John was very sick. _____ his illness, he went to work

      2. John was very sick. _____ his illness, he went to the hospital

   c. **Difficult living conditions** refers to the fact that

      1. Marya lived in a cold, uncomfortable apartment and ate little food

      2. Marya was a student and had to study hard

5. In July 1893, Marie passed her physics exam **first in her class. At this time,** she met Pierre Curie, a young scientist.

   a. What does **first in her class** mean?

      1. Marie graduated before all the other students.

      2. Marie was the best student in her class.

   b. **At this time** means

      1. at the same time she passed her exam

      2. in the 1890s

      3. during this time period

6. Marie and Pierre Curie discussed their work and the latest scientific events, such as the discovery of **X rays.**

   a. What are **X rays?**

   _____

   b. How do you know?

   _____

   c. This kind of information is called a

   _____

7. Pierre Curie stopped his own research **in order to** help Marie.

   a. Pierre Curie stopped his own research
      1. because he wanted to help Marie
      2. because he wanted to tell Marie what to do

   b. What follows **in order to?**
      1. An example
      2. A result
      3. A reason

8. Pierre realized that Marie was **about to** make an important discovery. **About to** means

   a. the time immediately before something happens
   b. the time immediately after something happens
   c. at the moment something is happening

9. In 1898, the Curies discovered two new elements that give off radiation. They named these elements polonium and radium. In those days, no one knew that **such radioactive materials** were dangerous.

   What does **such radioactive materials** refer to?

   _____

10. Marie Curie created the term **radioactivity** to describe these materials. This sentence means that

    a. Marie Curie was the first person to use the word *radioactivity*
    b. Marie Curie invented these radioactive materials

11. The Curies continued to work closely together **until** a **tragic** event occurred. On a rainy day in April, 1906, Pierre was killed in a street accident. Marie was **heartbroken,** but she continued working.

   a. **Until** means
      1. up to the time when something else happens
      2. up to the time when something else finishes

   b. Read the following sentences. Write the word **until** in the appropriate sentence.
      1. John studied very hard _____ he finished the exam.
      2. John studied very hard _____ the exam began.

   c. The word **tragic** means
      1. very violent
      2. very sad
      3. very surprising

   d. **Heartbroken** means that
      1. Marie was very unhappy
      2. Marie became very sick

12. **Over the years,** Marie's constant exposure to radiation continued to destroy her health.

   Over the years means

   a. in the years immediately before Marie died
   b. through all the years that she worked

13. Marie Curie's life had been one of hard work, **perseverance,** and self-sacrifice. However, in her personal life she was happy, and professionally, she achieved greatness in her **field.**

   a. Think about Marie Curie's life. What does the characteristic of **perseverance** mean?
      1. Marie Curie had a sad life.
      2. Marie Curie never stopped trying.
      3. Marie Curie had little money.

   b. What was Marie Curie's **field?**
      1. Paris
      2. Career
      3. Science

D. *Think* About It

Read the following questions and think about the answers. Write your answer below each question. Then, compare your answers with those of your classmates.

1. Marie Curie postponed, or delayed, her own education for six years so her older sister Bronya could attend medical school. Why do you think she did this?

   _____

2. How did Bronya repay Marie for Marie's support?

   _____

3. What kind of woman was Marie Curie? Write some adjectives that describe her.

   _____

4. Marie Curie never cared about making money. As a result, she sometimes worked under hard conditions. Do you agree with her philosophy? Explain your reasons.

   _____

E. DICTIONARY SKILLS

Read the dictionary entry for each word, and think about the context of the sentence. Write the number of the appropriate definition on the line next to the word. Then choose the sentence with the correct answer.

1.
> **support** *v.* **1** to hold up or bear the weight of: *a beam that supports a ceiling.* **2** to provide the money for necessities of life: *She supports her family by working two jobs.* **3** to contribute to; to encourage and assist by giving money to or working for: *We support our local hospital by giving blood regularly.* **4** to agree with, advocate, or express loyalty to: *He supports our efforts to end hunger in the world.* **5** to count in favor of: *The new findings support your theory.* **6** to work with: *This software supports all kinds of computers.*

Marya **supported** her older sister Bronya for six years while Bronya studied medicine at the Sorbonne in Paris.

a. **support:** _____

b. 1. Marya worked with Bronya while Bronya studied medicine at the Sorbonne.

2. Marya provided Bronya with money to live on while Bronya studied medicine at the Sorbonne.

2.
> **interrupt** *v.* **1** to stop s.t. from continuing: *A bad storm interrupted telephone communications between the two islands.* **2** to start talking or doing s.t. in the middle of s.o.'s conversation or activity, to break in: *Our little boy always interrupts our conversations by asking questions.* *-n.* [C;U] **interruption.**

After living with Bronya and her husband for a short time, Marie moved to an inexpensive apartment near the university so no one would **interrupt** her while she studied.

a. **interrupt:**

b. 1. Marie moved to an inexpensive apartment so no one would talk to her or disturb her while she studied.

2. Marie moved to an inexpensive apartment so no one could stop her from studying.

3.

> **constant** *adj.* **1** happening all the time, continuous: *I can't sleep because of the constant noise of the cars and trucks on the street.* **2** unchanging: *For 15 years, I have had a constant problem with a bad back.* **3** *frml.* faithful: *He is constant in his love for her.* *-n.* a quantity or quality that does not change: *In Rhode Island, the speed limit is a constant at 55 miles per hour.* *-adv.* **constantly.**

Marie's **constant** exposure to radiation over so many years eventually caused her death.

a. **constant:** _____

b. 1. Marie's unchanging exposure to radiation eventually caused her death.

2. Marie's faithful exposure to radiation eventually caused her death.

3. Marie's continuous exposure to radiation eventually caused her death.

4.

> **exposure** *n.* **1** [C;U] being unprotected, esp. from cold weather: *The lost mountain climbers suffered from exposure.* **2** [U] risk of loss: *We limit our exposure by investing only one quarter of the money.* **3** [C] a section of photographic film: *That roll of film contains 36 exposures.* **4** [C] a position or view in relation to a direction on the compass (north, south, east, or west): *The living room has a southern exposure.*

Marie's death was caused by her constant **exposure** to radiation over so many years.

a. **exposure:** _____

b. 1. Marie's death was caused by her risk of loss from radiation over so many years.

2. Marie's death was caused by her constantly being unprotected from radiation over so many years.

3. Marie's death was caused by her position in relation to radiation over so many years.

PART 1

In English, some verbs become nouns by adding the suffixes *-ance* or *-ence*, for example, *persist (v.), persistence (n.)*. Complete each sentence with the correct form of the word on the left. Be careful of spelling changes. **Write all the verbs in the past tense. The verbs may be affirmative or negative. The nouns may be singular or plural.**

occur *(v.)*
occurrence *(n.)*

1. a. Janet experienced several _____ of a serious illness before she began to get well.
    b. Finally, she felt well, her illness _____ again, and she was very happy.

exist *(v.)*
existence *(n.)*

2. a. For 100 years, no one could prove the _____ of a ninth planet in our solar system.
    b. Then, in 1930, Clyde Tombaugh proved that Pluto _____ when he located it through a telescope.

persevere *(v.)*
perseverance *(n.)*

3. a. Henry was having a lot trouble learning calculus, and he _____ because he became discouraged.
    b. Because he had no _____, he gave up, and failed his exams.

assist *(v.)*
assistance *(n.)*

4. a. When Andrew registered for classes, he needed some _____.
    b. Unfortunately, no one _____ him, and he filled out all the forms incorrectly.

assure *(v.)*
assurance *(n.)*

5. a. My brother Edward _____ me enough that plane travel is safe.
    b. Although he gave me many _____, I was very frightened on my first plane trip.

In English, some adjectives become nouns by adding the suffix *-ness,* for example, *sick (adj.), sickness (n.).* Complete each sentence with the correct form of the words on the left. **The nouns may be singular or plural.**

ill *(adj.)*
illness *(n.)*

1. a. It seems that Beverly is always _____.
   b. In fact, she has had four different _____ so far this year.

great *(adj.)*
greatness *(n.)*

2. a. Natalie has a reputation as a _____ tennis player.
   b. She has won many international competitions, and news of her _____ is spreading around the world.

happy *(adj.)*
happiness *(n.)*

3. a. Alex and Victoria's _____ is not accidental. They get along well, they have jobs they like, and they live in a comfortable home.
   b. Naturally, they are very _____ with their lives.

short *(adj.)*
shortness *(n.)*

4. a. It is a very _____ distance between Larry's house and the health club. It's just a five-minute walk.
   b. The _____ of the trip makes it convenient for Larry to exercise there every day.

near *(adj.)*
nearness *(n.)*

5. a. The shopping center is quite _____ Shirley's house.
   b. Because of the center's _____ to her home, she walks there to go shopping.

Read the following passage about Irene Curie, Marie and Pierre Curie's daughter. Then answer the questions which follow.

Irene Curie

Most people are aware that Marie Curie was the first woman to win the Nobel Prize, and the first person to win it twice. However, few people know that Marie Curie was also the mother of a Nobel Prize winner. Irene Curie was born on September 12, 1897. Irene was the first of Marie and Pierre Curie's two daughters. At the age of ten, Irene's talents and interest in mathematics were apparent. Irene, along with nine other children whose parents were also famous scholars, studied in their own school. It was known as the "Cooperative," and Marie Curie was one of their teachers. Irene finished her high school education at the College of Sevigne in Paris.

Irene entered the Sorbonne in October 1914 to prepare for a degree in mathematics and physics. When World War I began, Irene left the Sorbonne to help her mother, who was using X-ray facilities to help save the lives of wounded soldiers. Irene continued this work by developing X-ray facilities in military hospitals in France and Belgium. After the war, Irene received a Military Medal for her work.

In 1918, Irene became her mother's assistant at the Curie Institute. In December, 1924, Frederic Joliot visited the Institute, where he met Marie Curie. Frederic became one of her assistants, and Irene taught him the techniques required to work with radioactivity. Irene and Frederic soon fell in love and were married on October 29, 1926. Their daughter Helene was born on September 17, 1927, and their son Pierre on March 12, 1932. Like her mother, Irene combined family and career. Like her mother, Irene was awarded a Nobel prize, along with her husband Frederic, in 1935, for synthesizing new radioactive elements. Unfortunately, also like her mother, she developed leukemia because of her exposure to radiation. Irene Joliot-Curie died from leukemia on March 17, 1956.

QUESTIONS FOR ANOTHER LOOK

1. How was Irene Curie's education unusual?

    _____

    _____

2. Where did Irene meet her husband?

    _____

    _____

3. Why did Irene receive a Military Medal for her work?
    a. because she did scientific research
    b. because she helped the wounded soldiers
    c. because she received a degree in mathematics

4. Describe two ways that Irene and her mother, Marie Curie, were similar.

    _____

    _____

1. Go to the library and find out more information about Marie and Pierre's younger daughter, Eve. For example, when was she born? What did she do? Was she a scientist, too? Did she become well-known, too? Share your information with the class.

2. A biography is the story of a person's life. Prepare a biography of an important person from your country. Give an oral presentation of this person to your class.

3. Work in pairs or small groups. Make a list of the five most important discoveries of the twentieth century. Remember, a discovery is something a person *finds,* something that exists. An invention is something a person *creates,* such as the telephone, the light bulb, the automobile. Combine your list with the other groups' list. Together, choose the three most important discoveries.

I. **Topics** FOR *Discussion* AND *Writing*

1. a. What is a twentieth-century woman? How can you describe a twentieth-century woman?

    b. How does Marie Curie fit your description of a twentieth-century woman?

2. Marie Curie supported her sister Bronya when Bronya was in medical school. Then, when Bronya finished school, Marie began her own education. Why do you think Marie did this? What kind of person do you think she was? Would you support your sister or brother if you could? Explain your reasons.

3. Marie Curie made a lot of sacrifices for her work. She never made any money from her discoveries, and died from her life's work: radium. Do you know of any other individuals who sacrificed their lives for their work? Do you think you could sacrifice your life for your work? Why or why not? Explain your reasons.

4. Write your autobiography or the biography of someone you know personally and whom you admire.

5. **Write in your journal.** Work was the most important part of Marie Curie's life. Describe the most important part of your life at the present time. What do you think the most important part of your life will be in the future. Why?

Word Search

Read the words listed below. Find them in the puzzle and circle them. They may be written in any direction.

achieve	exposure	perseverance	support
discovery	field	radium	tragic
existence	heartbroken	scientist	unfortunately

```
D  B  D  C  S  L  B  E  N  D  V  L  U  X  T
H  T  C  U  U  E  X  I  S  T  E  N  C  E  T
D  B  F  M  P  T  A  V  H  P  F  H  J  Z  O
X  S  I  M  P  E  R  U  S  O  P  X  E  U  Z
Z  N  E  K  O  R  B  T  R  A  E  H  A  R  O
P  F  L  H  R  Q  E  T  Y  V  X  H  B  D  H
F  N  D  T  T  J  U  V  R  V  M  S  U  J  Z
N  O  X  E  C  N  A  R  E  V  E  S  R  E  P
Q  C  N  O  A  D  O  D  V  I  Y  J  V  D  Q
K  U  M  T  R  W  N  Q  O  U  H  O  T  C  Y
X  F  E  F  A  J  O  X  C  D  S  C  R  X  N
W  L  E  X  D  T  X  B  S  L  B  T  A  W  M
Y  R  S  C  I  E  N  T  I  S  T  Y  G  X  L
T  F  T  S  U  H  Y  X  D  I  Q  B  I  Y  N
X  P  Y  G  M  M  C  I  D  O  S  L  C  C  T
```

Crossword Puzzle

Read the clues on the next page. Write the answers in the correct spaces in the puzzle.

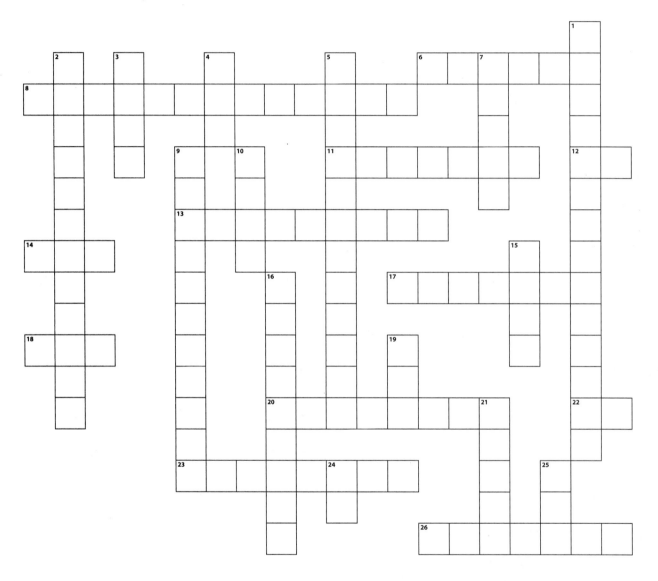

Crossword Puzzle Clues

Across Clues

6. A death is a very _____ occurrence.

8. Unhappily; unluckily

11. Give someone money to help him or her live or go to school

12. **I, _____; he, him**

13. When you find something for the first time, you make a _____.

14. Past participle of **put**

17. Sickness

18. Past participle of **hit**

20. Polonium, radium, gold, and iron are all _____.

22. The opposite of **yes**

23. _____ to X rays or to the sun's rays can cause injury to the body.

26. After a long time

Down Clues

1. Achievement

2. Something that causes a break in your work is an _____.

3. Past participle of **go**

4. Past participle of **run**

5. If you do not give up easily, you have _____.

7. The Nobel Prize is an important _____.

9. Polonium, radium, uranium, and plutonium are all _____ elements.

10. Past participle of **lose**

15. Past participle of **lend**

16. Harmful

19. _____, two, three, four

21. Past participle of **show**

24. The opposite of **down**

25. Every

Grammar Cloze Quiz

he	she	they
his	her	their

Read the passage below. Complete each blank space with one of the pronouns listed above. You may use the pronouns more than once.

In 1891, 23-year-old Marya Sklodowska went to Paris to begin _____ (1) education. Once _____ (2) arrived in Paris, Marya changed _____ (3) name to the French form, Marie. After living with Bronya and _____ (4) husband for a short time, _____ (5) moved near the university so _____ (6) could study without interruption. Marie's student life was extremely poor, but in spite of _____ (7) difficult living conditions, _____ (8) was happy.

In July 1893, Marie passed _____ (9) physics examination, first in _____ (10) class. At this time _____ (11) met Pierre Curie. _____ (12) was a young scientist. Marie and Pierre discovered that _____ (13) had much in common. _____ (14) both believed that science was the most important part of _____ (15) lives. _____ (16) fell in love and were married on July 26, 1895.

Marie and Pierre Curie were very happy. _____ (17) discussed _____ (18) work and the latest scientific events. Marie began to do research on X rays. Pierre Curie stopped _____ (19) own research in order to help Marie in _____ (20) work. _____ (21) realized that _____ (22) was about to make an important discovery.

1. Marie Curie won two Nobel Prizes for her achievements in science. Do you think Marie Curie's work agrees with Alfred Nobel's idea of special achievement? Explain your answer.

2. Would you like to win a Nobel Prize? How? In what category? Nobel Prize winners receive approximately $1 million in prize money. What would you do with the money?

1. The video is about Albert Einstein, a great scientist and Nobel Prize winner. Have you heard of Einstein? What is he famous for?

2. Read the questions and then watch the video once or twice. Put a check on the line next to the correct answers.

   a. Einstein is considered one of the most _____ scientific thinkers in history.

   _____ old-fashioned _____ brilliant _____ constant

   b. In the early 1900's Einstein invented the Theory of

   _____ Relativity _____ Relatives _____ Relationships

   c. What two inventions help to support Einstein's theory?

   _____ Atomic clocks _____ Quasars _____ Lasers _____ Galaxies

   d. Einstein's theory proved that gravity can _____ light.

   _____ block _____ brighten _____ bend

   e. Einstein received a Nobel Prize in _____.

   _____ Literature _____ Physics _____ Medicine _____ Peace

3. What do Marie Curie and Albert Einstein have in common?

Surfing THE *INTERNET*

Using Google, Excite, Netscape, Yahoo or another search engine, type the key words "Nobel Prize" and read more about the prize, Einstein, or Marie Curie. One good site for research is http://www.almaz.com/nobel

Optional Activity: Look up the name of another famous scientist such as George Washington Carver, Stephen Hawking, Rosalind Franklin, or Linus Pauling. Tell the class what this scientist did to influence the world of science.

UNIT 6

THE EARTH'S RESOURCES AND DANGERS

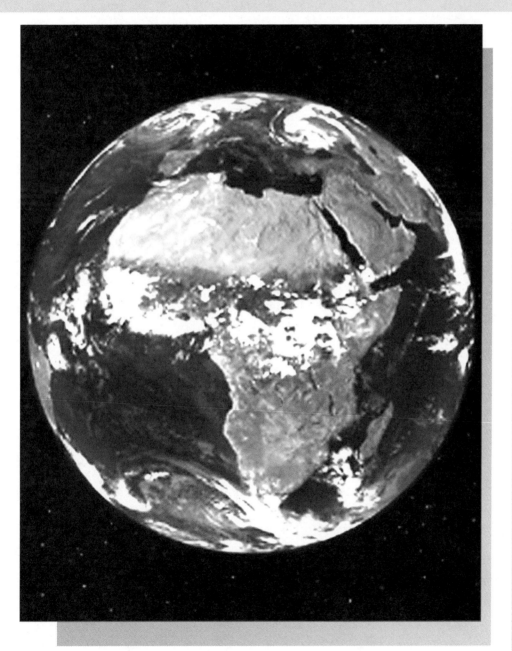

Oil as an Important World Resource

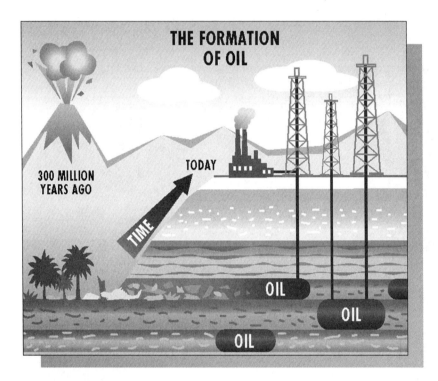

Prereading Preparation

1. Work with a partner to make a list of some uses of oil for the home and transportation.

USES OF OIL	
Transportation	Home

2. Look at the illustration above. Then read the paragraph on the next page. Complete the following flowchart on page 227, using information from both.

The Formation of Oil

Oil is usually called petroleum. Petroleum is very complex, but it is made up of only two elements: carbon (C) and hydrogen (H). Together, carbon and hydrogen are called hydrocarbons. Hydrocarbons are the remains of ancient plants and animals. These plants and animals lived and died millions of years ago. When they died, they were covered by mud, and bacteria broke down the organic remains. Over thousands of years, more plants and animals died and were covered by more mud. The weight of the upper layers and the heat from the pressure eventually changed the mud into solid rock, called sedimentary rock. It also changed the organic material into oil and natural gas.

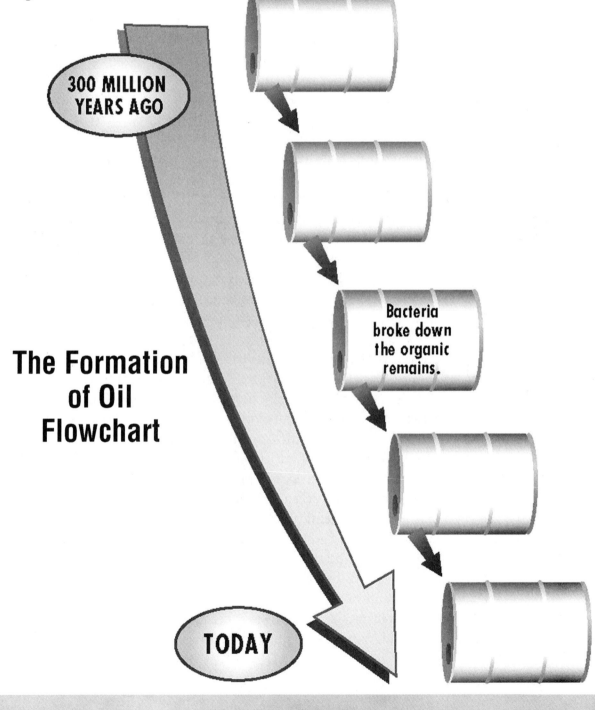

300 MILLION YEARS AGO

The Formation of Oil Flowchart

Bacteria broke down the organic remains.

TODAY

Oil as an Important World Resource

1   We may not realize it, but oil is an essential part of our everyday lives. Oil, which is usually called petroleum, is a valuable world resource because of the many useful products that are manufactured from it. In fact, petroleum is the most important substance we use in modern society, next to food. The process
5   of manufacturing petroleum products begins when oil is first taken out of the ground.

When petroleum first comes out of the ground, it is called crude oil. This oil is impure. In other words, it is dirty, and people need to clean, or refine, it. First, the oil goes into a furnace to heat it. When the oil is heated, it separates
10   into lighter and heavier parts. For example, the lightest part of the oil becomes natural gas. We use natural gas to heat our homes and cook with. The heaviest part of the oil becomes asphalt. We use asphalt to pave roads and parking lots. In between the natural gas and the asphalt, this process produces gasoline, kerosene, heating oil, and lubricating oil. We use lubricating oil to grease
15   machines and other metal objects with moving parts, for example, sewing machines. However, these are just a few of the 6,000 petroleum products, or petrochemicals, that are manufactured from crude oil. Petrochemicals are used in almost every area of our lives, including housing, clothing, and personal use, as well as medicine and transportation.

20   In the past, people's homes contained only natural materials, such as wool or cotton carpets, and wood furniture. Today, however, furniture, furniture fabrics, carpeting, paint, and wallpaper are all made from petroleum-based synthetics. We heat our homes with oil or natural gas instead of wood. In the past 50 years, our clothes have been made from synthetic fibers such as rayon,
25   nylon, polyester, Orlon, Dacron, and acetate. Today, clothing is even made from used plastic containers, which are also petrochemical products. The detergent we use to wash dishes and clean our clothes are petroleum-based products, as are children's toys, shampoo, lipstick, and hand lotion.

Petrochemicals have a wide variety of medical uses. The vitamins we take
30   and some of the drugs that our doctors prescribe are made of petrochemicals. For example, today's aspirin and other synthetic pain relievers such as acetaminophen are petrochemical products. Cold medicines that relieve our stuffy noses and drugs that help some people breathe more easily are, too.

The transportation industry is very dependent on petrochemicals. We all
35   know that gasoline, kerosene, and diesel oil provide fuel for cars, motorcycles, trucks, airplanes, and ships. However, not everyone is aware that cars and trucks are made of petrochemicals, too. For instance, car and truck bodies are made of hundreds of pounds of polyester. Bumpers are no longer made of steel, and tires

40

are synthetic, not real, rubber. Seat covers are vinyl. Traffic lights, road signs, and the painted lines on roads are all made of petrochemicals.

Although the world supply of petroleum is limited, and will one day run out, for now we have an adequate supply to meet the world's needs. Petrochemical products will remain an essential part of our lives for many years to come.

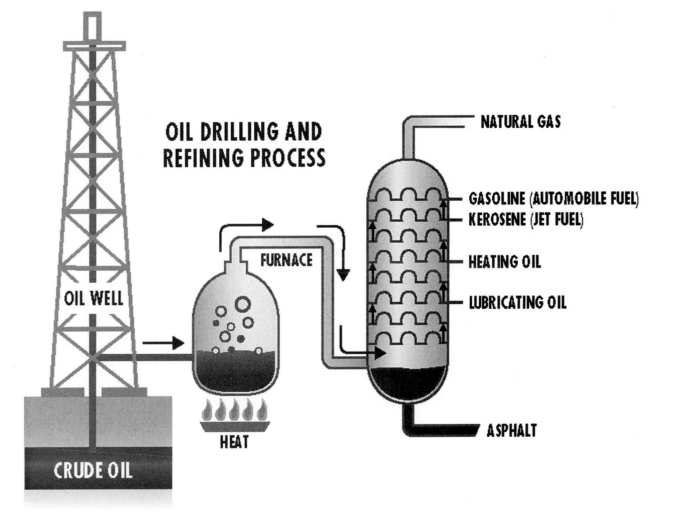

OIL DRILLING AND REFINING PROCESS

OIL WELL

CRUDE OIL

FURNACE

HEAT

NATURAL GAS

GASOLINE (AUTOMOBILE FUEL)
KEROSENE (JET FUEL)

HEATING OIL

LUBRICATING OIL

ASPHALT

Read the passage once. Then read the following statements. Check whether they are True or False. If a statement is false, change the statement so that it is true. Then go back to the passage and find the line that supports your answer.

1. _____ True _____ False   Petroleum is another word for oil.

_____

2. _____ True _____ False   Crude oil does not need to be cleaned.

_____

3. _____ True _____ False   The lightest part of the oil becomes natural gas.

_____

4. _____ True _____ False   Kerosene is heavier than asphalt.

_____

5. _____ True _____ False   Our homes contain many products made of petrochemicals.

_____

6. _____ True _____ False   Petrochemicals have no medical uses.

_____

7. _____ True _____ False   We all use and depend on petroleum products.

_____

B.   Skimming and Scanning Exercise

PART 1

Skim through the passage. Then read the following statements. Choose the one that is the correct main idea of the reading.

a. Petroleum is dirty when it comes from the ground and needs to be cleaned.

b. Heating crude oil separates it into lighter and heavier parts.

c. Petroleum is an important natural resource that has many essential uses.

PART 2

Scan the passage. Work with a partner to fill in the chart below with information from the reading.

USES OF PETROLEUM					
Housing	Clothing	Personal Uses	Medical Uses	Transportation	Other Uses

Reading Analysis

Read each question carefully. Either circle the letter of the correct answer or write your answer in the space provided.

1. Oil, which is usually called **petroleum,** is a valuable world resource because of the many useful products that are manufactured from it. **In fact,** petroleum is the most important substance we use in modern society, **next to** food.

   a. What is a synonym for **petroleum?**

   _____

   b. The sentence after **in fact**
      1. is the same as the sentence before it, but in different words
      2. emphasizes the information before it
      3. is a different idea from the information before it

   c. Complete the following sentence with the appropriate choice. Yesterday was a very cold day. In fact,
      1. I had to wear a heavy coat
      2. it snowed all day long
      3. the temperature was 10°F below zero

   d. Petroleum is the most important substance we use in modern society, **next to** food.

      In modern society, which substance is the most important: petroleum or food?

      _____

2. When petroleum first comes out of the ground, it is called crude oil. This oil is **impure. In other words,** it is dirty, and people need to clean, or **refine,** it.

   a. What does **impure** mean?
      1. Oil
      2. Dirty
      3. From the ground

b. What type of information follows **in other words?**
   1. An example
   2. Additional information
   3. The same information in different words

c. What does **refine** mean?

   _____

d. How do you know?

   _____

3. Gasoline, kerosene, and asphalt are just a few of the 6,000 petroleum products, or **petrochemicals,** that are manufactured from crude oil. Petrochemicals are used in almost every area of our lives, including housing, clothing, and personal use, **as well as** medicine and transportation.

a. What are **petrochemicals?**

   _____

b. What does **as well as** mean?
   1. Very good
   2. Equal to
   3. In addition to

4. In the past, people's homes contained only **natural** materials, such as wool or cotton carpets, and wood furniture. Today, however, furniture, furniture fabrics, carpeting, paint, and wallpaper are all made from petroleum-based **synthetics.**

a. What are examples of **natural** materials?

   _____

b. What are **synthetic** materials?
   1. Artificial; manmade
   2. Materials for home use

5. The **detergents** we use to wash dishes and clean our clothes are petroleum-based products, **as are** children's toys, shampoo, lipstick, and hand lotion.

    a. **Detergent** is

        1. a kind of machine

        2. a kind of soap

        3. a kind of process

    b. In this sentence, **as are** means

        1. children's toys, shampoo, lipstick, and hand lotion are petroleum-based products, too

        2. children's toys, shampoo, lipstick, and hand lotion are washed with detergent, too

6. Some of the drugs that our doctors **prescribe** are made of petrochemicals. For example, today's aspirin and other synthetic pain **relievers** such as acetaminophen are petrochemical products.

    a. When doctors **prescribe** medicine, they

        1. sell medicine to us

        2. make medicine for us

        3. order the use of a specific medicine

    b. A pain **reliever** is a drug that

        1. lessens our pain

        2. is synthetic

7. Car and truck **bodies** are made of hundreds of pounds of polyester. Car and truck **bodies** are

    a. people in cars and trucks

    b. the front, back, sides, and doors of cars and trucks

    c. people that cars and trucks hit and kill

8. Although the world supply of petroleum is limited, and will one day **run out,** for now we have an **adequate** supply to meet the world's needs. Petrochemical products will remain an essential part of our lives for many years to come.

   a. One day the world supply of petroleum

      1. will be part of our lives

      2. will not be necessary

      3. will end

   b. **Adequate** means

      1. expensive

      2. enough

      3. useful

D. *Think* About It

Read the following questions and think about the answers. Write your answer below each question. Then, compare your answers with those of your classmates.

1. Besides oil, what is another valuable natural resource that is essential to our lives? Why is this natural resource essential?

   _____

2. How do you think everyday life in the past was different without oil? Was it easier or more difficult? Please explain your answer.

   _____

3. What are other sources of energy that people can use instead of oil?

   _____

E. DICTIONARY SKILLS

Read the dictionary entry for each word and think about the context of the sentence. Write the number of the appropriate definition on the line next to the word. In addition, circle *noun*, *adjective*, or *adverb* where indicated. Then choose the sentence with the correct answer.

1.

> **realize** *v.* **-ized, -izing, -izes** **1** to understand, start to believe s.t. is true, *(syn.)* to **recognize:** *He realizes now that he needs to go back to college for more education.* **2** to gain, make money: *The woman realized a profit from the sale of her house.* **3** to make s.t. become true, *(syn.)* to **accomplish:** *This summer I will realize my dream of going to Italy.*

We may not **realize** it, but oil is an essential part of our everyday lives. In fact, petroleum is the most important substance we use in modern society, next to food.

a. **realize:**

b. 1. We may not make any money from it, but oil is an essential part of our lives.

2. We may not understand it, but oil is an essential part of our lives.

3. We may not make it true, but oil is an essential part of our lives.

2.

> **essential** *adj.* **1** central, major: *The essential point is we must do what the contract says.* **2** necessary, required: *It is essential that you deliver the message this morning.* *-adv.* **essentially.** *-n.pl.* **the essentials:** the things necessary to s.t.: *The essentials of life are food, shelter, and clothing.*

We may not realize it, but oil is an **essential** part of our everyday lives. In fact, petrochemical products will remain an **essential** part of our lives for many years to come.

a. **essential:** _____ (adjective/noun)

b. 1. Oil is a major part of our everyday lives.

2. Oil is a required part of our everyday lives.

3.

> **substance** *n.* **1** [U] anything one can touch, material, matter: *This face cream is a white, sticky substance.* ‖ *Tires are made of rubber and other substances.* **2** *usu. sing.* [C;U] meaning, truth: *What she says has substance because of her knowledge and experience.* **3** [U] wealth, possessions: *The family owns a successful business; they are people of substance.*

Petroleum is the most important **substance** we use in modern society, next to food.

a. **substance:** _____

b. 1. Petroleum is the most important truth in modern society, next to food.

2. Petroleum is the most important wealth in modern society, next to food.

3. Petroleum is the most important material in modern society, next to food.

4.

> **wide** *adj.* **wider, widest** **1** related to the distance from side to side: *That table is three feet wide.* **2** with a great distance from side to side: *A long bridge crossed the wide river.* **3** large, *(syn.)* <u>extensive</u>: *She can play a wide range of musical instruments: the piano, guitar, and trumpet.* -*adv.* **1** completely, fully: *wide-open* ‖ *wide-awake* **2** **wide of the mark:** away from the target: *The arrow missed the center; it was wide of the mark.* -*fig.* wrong, incorrect: *His answer to the question was wide of the mark.* -*suffix* **-wide:** extending over or all through an area: *The position of governor is a statewide elective office.* -*adv.* **widely;** -*n.* **wideness.**

Petrochemicals have a **wide** variety of medical uses. For example, the vitamins we take and some of the drugs that our doctors prescribe are made of petrochemicals.

a. **wide:** _____ (adjective/adverb)

b. 1. Petrochemicals have an extensive variety of medical uses.

2. Petrochemicals have a distant variety of medical uses.

3. Petrochemicals have a side-to-side variety of medical uses.

5.

> **aware** *adj.* **1** conscious of, alert to: *He is out of the coma, but he can't speak. He is aware of people around him, though.* **2** knowledgeable about, understanding of: *A newspaper reporter must be aware of current events.* -*n.* [U] **awareness.**

We all know that gasoline, kerosene, and diesel oil provide fuel for cars, motorcycles, trucks, airplanes, and ships. However, not everyone is **aware** that cars and trucks are made of petrochemicals, too.

a. **aware:** _____

b. 1. Not everyone is conscious of the fact that cars and trucks are made of petrochemicals.

2. Not everyone is knowledgeable of the fact that cars and trucks are made of petrochemicals.

PART 1

In English, some verbs become nouns by adding the suffix *-tion,* for example, *create (v.), creation (n.).* If the word ends in *e,* the *e* is dropped. Furthermore, sometimes the word changes in spelling. Complete each sentence with the correct form of the word on the left. **Write all the verbs in the simple present tense. They may be affirmative or negative. The nouns may be singular or plural.**

produce *(v.)*
production *(n.)*

1. a. Australia _____ very much petroleum or natural gas.
    b. In fact, Australia's yearly _____ of oil and gas is the lowest in the world.

prescribe *(v.)*
prescription *(n.)*

2. a. Doctors are the only people who can write _____ for certain drugs that can be dangerous.
    b. However, doctors _____ basic drugs such as aspirin. We can buy them without a prescription.

transport *(v.)*
transportation *(n.)*

3. a. Petroleum companies _____ oil by airplane. They ship oil in large tankers, or ships.
    b. The _____ of oil is also done by pipeline, for example, in the state of Alaska.

lubricate *(v.)*
lubrication *(n.)*

4. a. Monica takes good care of her bicycle. She carefully _____ the gears and the chain every month.
    b. She uses a high-quality oil for proper _____.

add *(v.)*
addition *(n.)*

5. a. Bill and Arthur always _____ the figures on their check when they eat in a restaurant.
    b. Occasionally a waiter makes mistakes when he does his _____, so Bill and Arthur like to make sure the total is correct.

PART 2

In English, the noun form and the verb form of some words are the same, for example, *drill (v.)*, *drill (n.)*. Complete each sentence with the correct form of the word on the left. Circle (v.) if you are using the verb, or (n.) if you are using the noun form of each word. **Write all the verbs in the single present tense. They may be affirmative or negative. The nouns may be singular or plural.**

supply

1. a. Many countries now _____ the world with natural
      (v., n.)
      gas and oil, but these reserves are limited.

   b. At some time in the next 100 years, the world's entire
      _____ of oil and gas will end, and all countries will
      (v., n.)
      need other sources of energy.

grease

2. a. There are many different types of _____ for vari-
      ous purposes.   *(v., n.)*

   b. For example, whenever Fred _____ his car, he
      (v., n.)
      uses different lubricants for different parts of his car.

heat

3. a. In many countries of the world, people _____
      (v., n.)
      their homes with oil or gas. They use wood or coal instead.

   b. The amount of _____ that a house gets is usually
      (v., n.)
      controlled with an instrument called a thermostat.

process

4. a. Numerous _____ are involved in the oil-refining
      industry.   *(v., n.)*

   b. However, most oil companies _____ crude oil in
      the same manner.   *(v., n.)*

fuel

5. a. People _____ their cars with gasoline, but trucks
      (v., n.)
      usually use diesel oil.

   b. Airplanes do not use either gasoline or diesel. The
      _____ they use is kerosene or jet fuel.
      (v., n.)

Read the following story, then answer the questions.

The DO IT Homestead

Charlie and Fran Collins live in southwest Utah on the family farm which they built together. For the last 21 years, the Collinses have not paid any electrical bills. They have run their home and their farm completely on solar energy. They do not depend on electrical companies to supply their power.

Many people dream of becoming energy self-sufficient for different reasons. Some people want to use energy sources that are safer for the environment, or environmentally friendly. However, while most of us only dream about becoming energy self-sufficient, Charlie and Fran Collins actually did it. When the Collinses bought their 240-acre farm, they began experimenting with various sources of light and energy. After 21 years, they have a lifestyle that has all of the modern conveniences, but which is powered entirely on solar energy. The Collinses call their home "The Do It Homestead," because Charlie and Fran understood that if they wanted to get anything done, they had to "DO IT" themselves.

Using 24 solar electric panels, the Collinses produce enough electricity to meet their needs for three to five days with no sunlight. They run lights, a solar refrigerator/freezer, and other household appliances, such as a dishwasher, washing machine, and vacuum cleaner.

Charlie's dream is to help others become as self-reliant as he and his wife are on their Utah homestead. He is the author of "Ask Mr. Solar," a popular newspaper column that answers people's questions about solar energy. Charlie and Fran Collins also teach a college course about solar energy through the Internet. For people who are interested in alternative energy, the Collinses are experienced sources of information. The knowledge they have can be invaluable to anyone who dreams of providing power to their homes without having to pay monthly electric bills.

QUESTIONS FOR ANOTHER LOOK

1. How do the Collinses run their home and farm?

    _____

2. Why are the Collinses *energy self-sufficient?*
    a. They built their own farm.
    b. They do not rely on electrical companies for power.
    c. They do not use any source of energy.

3. What is one reason why some people want to be energy self-sufficient?

    _____

    _____

4. Complete the following sentence:

    The Collinses call their farm the "Do It Homestead" because _____

    _____

5. The Collinses can give you information if you want to become energy self-sufficient because
    a. they have been energy self-sufficient for 21 years
    b. Mr. Collins writes a newspaper column about solar energy
    c. the Collinses teach a college course about solar energy
    d. All of the above

Follow-Up Activities

1. Make a list of the ways you use petrochemical products in your life. When you are finished, compare your list with a classmate's list. What products did you list which were not mentioned in the passage?

MY USES OF PETROLEUM-BASED PRODUCTS					
Housing	Clothing	Personal Uses	Medical Uses	Transportation	Other Uses

2. Refer to the WORLD OIL RESERVES bar graph below. Write the answers to the following questions.

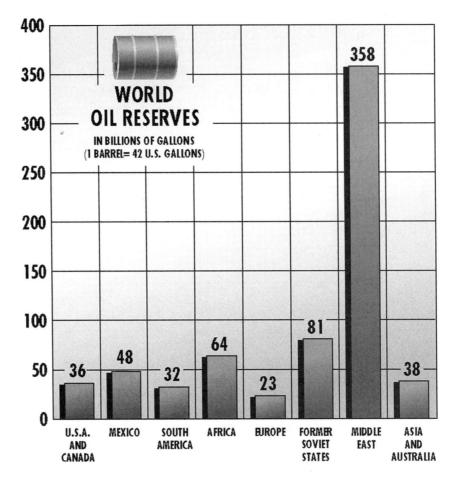

a. Which country or area has the largest oil reserves in the world?

_____

b. Which country or area has the smallest oil reserves in the world?

_____

c. Which country or area has the second-largest oil reserves in the world?

_____

d. Which one of the following statements is true?

    1. The Middle East has smaller oil reserves than all the other countries and areas combined.

    2. The Middle East has the same amount of oil reserves as all of the other countries and areas combined.

    3. The Middle East has bigger oil reserves than all of the other countries and areas combined.

I. Topics FOR Discussion AND Writing

1. Think about people's lives at home, at work, at school, etc. Describe how oil makes life easier for people.

2. The reading passage explains the process of changing oil into different products. Think of another process where something is changed into a useful product. Describe the process, for example, how people change wood into paper.

3. There are many other scientific advances that make life better or easier for us. Work with a classmate and make a list. Then select one and describe it.

4. **Write in your journal.** Imagine there is no more oil in the world. Describe a day in your life without oil.

Read the words listed below. Find them in the puzzle and circle them. They may be written in any direction.

adequate	fuel	prescription	refine
aware	heat	process	synthetic
essential	lubricate	realize	transportation

```
N  O  I  T  A  T  R  O  P  S  N  A  R  T  E
Q  A  Y  Z  H  Q  Z  D  R  T  C  E  J  S  G
W  V  D  B  E  P  F  S  E  A  T  Q  S  L  D
R  M  G  T  L  W  U  Z  S  A  H  E  A  T  C
S  Y  N  T  H  E  T  I  C  E  N  V  A  V  G
R  E  W  A  M  D  U  I  R  T  C  J  W  B  B
E  M  T  G  F  J  R  F  I  H  J  O  A  Q  C
F  Z  G  A  V  B  P  A  P  O  H  C  R  C  H
I  C  I  J  U  D  L  N  T  Q  W  V  E  P  Z
N  G  W  L  E  Q  A  U  I  G  I  S  Y  D  L
E  G  Y  W  A  K  E  H  O  O  P  J  X  A  I
V  X  O  V  Q  E  G  D  N  C  F  N  I  F  M
A  O  A  E  Q  D  R  G  A  A  S  G  J  B  I
```

Crossword Puzzle

Read the clues on the next page. Write the answers in the correct pages in the puzzle.

Crossword Puzzle Clues

Across Clues

1. Women put _____ on their lips for color.

4. I use a _____ to unlock my door when I come home.

6. Past participle of **run**

7. We need to _____ the moving parts of machines.

11. Nylon is a _____ fiber. Cotton is a natural fiber.

13. When I meet my friend, I _____ hello.

14. _____ are oil-based products.

17. Quiz; exam

18. We use _____ to clean our clothes.

19. John likes tea. I like tea, _____.

20. I will wait _____ you after class.

21. We use _____ to lubricate the moving parts of machines.

23. We use _____ to pave our highways and parking lots. It is black and heavy oil.

24. Food is the most important _____ in our lives, but oil is an important _____, too.

25. The opposite of **lose**

26. We _____ dishes in the kitchen sink.

27. Susan hasn't eaten lunch _____. It's only 10 o'clock.

28. Children love to play with _____.

Down Clues

2. Unclean, dirty

3. He _____ a good math student.

4. _____ is the fuel that airplanes use. They do not use gasoline.

5. Today, many containers are made of _____ instead of glass.

8. The opposite of **girl**

9. I _____ speak two languages.

10. Natural gas is the _____ part of processed oil. Gasoline is heavier.

12. **She, _____ , it**

14. Another word for **oil**

15. Oil is a mixture of two elements. Together, these two elements are called _____.

16. Automobiles

19. The opposite of **bottom**

20. Cotton and wool are natural _____.

22. Purify; clean

26. You and I

| is | are | was | were |

Read the passage below. Complete each blank space with a form of *be* listed above. You may use the words more than once.

In the past, carpets and furniture _____ made from natural (1)
materials, like cotton and wood. Today, however, furniture, furniture fabrics, carpeting, paint, and wallpaper _____ all made from petroleum- (2)
based synthetics. Our homes _____ heated with oil or natural (3)
gas instead of wood. These days some clothing _____ even (4)
made from used plastic containers. These containers _____ also (5)
petrochemical products. The soap we use to clean our clothes

_____ also a petroleum-based product, but in the past soap (6)
_____ made from animal fat. (7)

Petrochemicals have a wide variety of medical uses. Some of the drugs that our doctors prescribe _____ made of petrochemicals. For (8)
example, today's aspirin _____ a petrochemical product. Cold (9)
medicines that help some people breathe more easily _____ too. (10)

12

How Earthquakes Happen

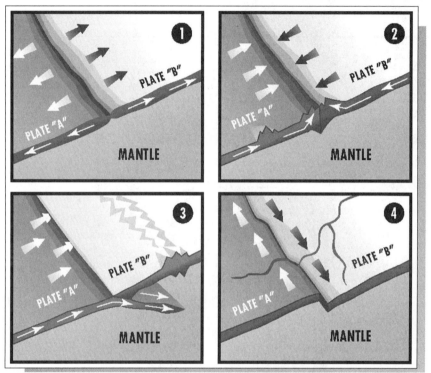

1. Where in the world do earthquakes occur? Do they occur in your country?

2. Look at the illustration. It shows how earthquakes occur. Read the paragraph below. Using information from both the paragraph and the illustration, fill in the flowchart which follows.

How Earthquakes Occur

1   The earth's crust, or surface, is made of rock. The crust covers the earth, but it is not in one piece. It is broken into a number of large pieces called plates. These plates are always moving because they lie on top of liquid rock. They slide over the hot, melted rock. The plates move very slowly in different directions.
5   The difference in motion causes the earth's crust to break. This is an earthquake. Earthquakes happen in different ways. In some areas of the earth, the plates move apart. This happens in the middle of the Atlantic Ocean. Earthquakes also take place inside of plates throughout the world. For example, China is being squeezed in two directions, from the east by the Pacific plate and from the south
10   by the India-Australia plate. In other places, plates push directly against each other, and one plate moves downward under the other plate. For instance, this happens off the western coasts of South and Central America and off the coast of Japan. The plates are sliding past one another in other regions of the world, for example, at the San Andreas fault zone in California.

FLOWCHART: HOW EARTHQUAKES OCCUR

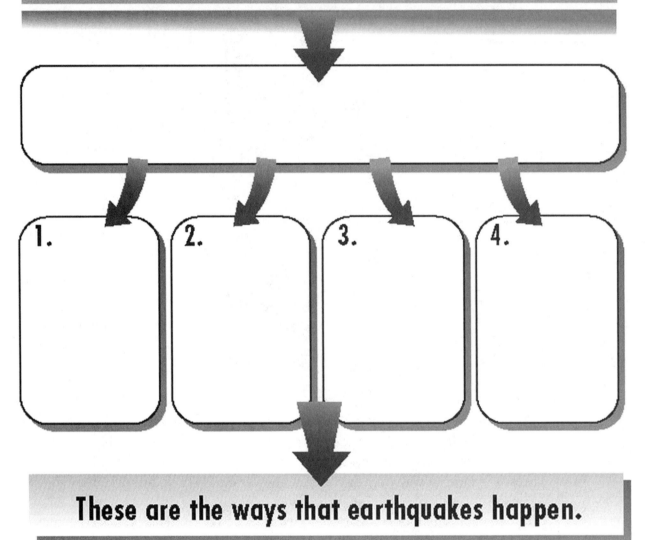

The Earth's plates slide over hot, melted rock.

1.

2.

3.

4.

These are the ways that earthquakes happen.

How Earthquakes Happen

1   Earthquake! People all around the world fear earthquakes because they cause so much destruction and death. Consider the following facts: The Northridge earthquake struck the San Fernando Valley region of Southern California on January 17, 1994. The earthquake caused 57 deaths, over 5,000
5   injuries, and extensive building damage. In fact, some people estimate that the earthquake caused millions of dollars in property damage. The Northridge earthquake ranks as one of the worst natural disasters in the U.S. history.

      On January 17, 1995, the Hyogoken-Nanbu (Kobe) earthquake struck south-central Japan. This earthquake resulted in over 5,400 deaths and many thousands
10   of injuries. The damage costs were estimated at 150 billion U.S. dollars. Although this earthquake was only rated as a moderate-to-large earthquake, it caused so much destruction because it produced a fault break directly through the business area of a city.

      These statistics are very frightening. Many people wonder if the number of
15   earthquakes is increasing. In reality, the number of earthquakes has actually decreased in recent years. However, because of improved world communication, people receive more news and information than ever before. For example, in the last 20 years, we have been able to locate more earthquakes yearly because there are more seismograph, or earthquake measuring, stations in the world. These
20   additional stations help seismological centers to locate many small earthquakes which were undetectable years ago.

      Many scientists are trying to predict earthquakes, but these predictions are very uncertain. Scientists cannot calculate the exact location, time, or intensity of an earthquake. Furthermore, the predicted earthquake may not take place at
25   all. As a result, scientists do not think it is a useful idea to announce that an earthquake will take place on a specific day. Instead, most people are trying to design structures such as buildings, dams, and bridges that can resist earthquakes. People can reduce loss of life, injuries, and property damage by sufficiently preparing themselves, their homes, work places, and communities for
30   a major earthquake. After all, it is possible to survive an earthquake.

Fact-Finding Exercise

Read the passage once. Then read the following statements. Check whether they are True or False. If a statement is false, change the sentence so that it is true. Then go back to the passage and find the line that supports your answer.

1. ＿＿ True ＿＿ False   The earthquake damage in Kobe was more costly than the earthquake damage in Northridge.

_____

2. ＿＿ True ＿＿ False   More people were killed in the earthquake in Northridge than were killed in the earthquake in Kobe.

_____

3. ＿＿ True ＿＿ False   In recent years, the number of earthquakes has increased.

_____

4. ＿＿ True ＿＿ False   There are more seismological centers in the world today than there were in the past.

_____

5. ＿＿ True ＿＿ False   Scientists cannot predict when an earthquake will occur.

_____

6. ＿＿ True ＿＿ False   We cannot protect ourselves from earthquakes.

_____

Skimming and Scanning Exercise

PART 1

Skim through the passage. Then read the following statements. Choose the one that is the correct main idea of the reading.

a. Earthquakes, which occur all over the world, cause death, injuries, and destruction, and are very difficult to predict.

b. Earthquakes occur all over the world, but we can protect ourselves if we are prepared.

c. There are many seismological centers all over the world that can tell us when an earthquake occurs.

PART 2

Scan the passage. Work with a partner to fill in the chart below with information from the reading.

Earthquakes			
Place	Number of Injuries	Number of Deaths	Cost of Damage
Northridge			
Kobe			
Ways to reduce the possibility of earthquake damage			

Read each question carefully. Either circle the letter of the correct answer, or write your answer in the space provided.

1. People all around the world fear earthquakes because they cause so much destruction and death. **Consider the following facts:** The Northridge earthquake struck the San Fernando Valley region of Southern California on January 17, 1994. The earthquake caused 57 deaths, **over 5,000 injuries,** and extensive building damage. **In fact,** some people estimate that the earthquake caused millions of dollars in property damage. The Northridge earthquake ranks as **one of the worst natural disasters in U.S. history.**

   a. **Consider the following facts** means
      1. think about this information
      2. remember this information
      3. be afraid of this information

   b. **"...over 5,000 injuries"** means
      1. exactly 5,000 people were hurt
      2. more than 5,000 people were hurt
      3. fewer than 5,000 people were hurt

   c. What information follows **in fact?**
      1. Different information that introduces a new idea
      2. Additional information that gives more details about the previous sentence
      3. True information that everyone believes

   d. How does the Northridge earthquake rank as a U.S. natural disaster?
      1. Very bad, but not the worst
      2. The worst

e. Which of the following can also be natural disasters?
   1. Car accidents
   2. Hurricanes
   3. Floods
   4. House fires
   5. Tornadoes
   6. Forest fires
   7. Murders

2. On January 17, 1995, the Hyogoken-Nanbu (Kobe) earthquake struck south-central Japan. This earthquake resulted in over 5,400 deaths and many thousands of injuries. **The damage costs were estimated at 150 billion U.S. dollars.**

   The estimated damage was

   a. a little less than $150 billion
   b. approximately $150 billion
   c. more than $150 billion

3. **These statistics are very frightening.** Many people wonder if the number of earthquakes is actually increasing. **In reality,** the number of earthquakes has actually decreased in recent years.

   a. What are **"these statistics?"**
      1. The number of earthquakes that happen every year in California and Japan
      2. The number of people who died in earthquakes in the last few years in California and Japan
      3. The number of deaths and injuries, and the amount of destruction caused by the earthquakes in Kobe and California

   b. What information follows **in reality?**
      1. True information which shows that the information in the previous sentence was correct
      2. True information which shows that the information in the previous sentence is incorrect
      3. Additional information that gives more details about the previous sentence

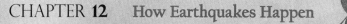

4. In the last 20 years, we have been able to locate more earthquakes yearly because there are more seismographic, or earthquake-measuring, stations in the world. These additional stations help seismological centers to locate many small earthquakes which were **undetectable** years ago.

a. What does a **seismographic measuring station** do?

_____

b. **Undetectable** means
   1. unnoticeable
   2. lost
   3. unimportant

5. Many scientists are trying to predict earthquakes, but these predictions are very uncertain. Scientists cannot **calculate** the exact location, time, or intensity of an earthquake. **Furthermore,** the **predicted** earthquake may not take place at all.

a. **Predict** means
   1. stop something from happening.
   2. tell something will happen before it happens.
   3. understand something by reading about it.

b. **Calculate** means
   1. tell everyone
   2. see
   3. figure out

c. What information comes after **furthermore?**
   1. More information about the same subject
   2. The same information in different words
   3. The result of the information before **furthermore**

6. Many scientists are trying to predict earthquakes, but these predictions are very uncertain. The predicted earthquake may not take place at all. **As a result,** they do not think it is a useful idea to announce that an earthquake will take place on a specific day.

   a. Why don't scientists think it is a useful idea to announce that an earthquake will take place?
      1. Because they don't want people to protect themselves
      2. Because they are not sure what time the earthquake will occur
      3. Because the predicted earthquake might not take place at all

   b. Finish the following sentence with the correct selection.
      Elizabeth read several interesting books about earthquakes. **As a result,**
      1. she became a better reader
      2. she decided to live in California
      3. she learned many new facts about earthquakes

   c. **As a result** means
      1. moreover
      2. consequently
      3. however

7. Scientists do not think it is a useful idea to announce that an earthquake will take place on a specific day. **Instead,** more people are trying to design structures such as buildings, dams, and bridges that can **resist** earthquakes.

   a. **Instead** introduces
      1. an idea that is similar to the previous idea
      2. an idea that gives more details about the previous idea
      3. an idea that takes the place of the previous idea

   b. A building that can **resist** an earthquake
      1. will fall down
      2. will not fall down

D. *Think* About It

Read the following questions and think about the answers. Write your answer below each question. Then, compare your answers with those of your classmates.

1. Some areas of the earth experience earthquakes often, especially places such as California and Japan. Why do people continue to live where earthquakes are likely to take place?

   _____

2. Scientists do not think it is a good idea to announce an earthquake because it may not actually take place. Do you agree with the scientists? Explain your answer.

   _____

   _____

3. What other natural disasters do people need to prepare themselves for? How can they prepare for these disasters?

   _____

   _____

E. DICTIONARY SKILLS

Read the dictionary entry for each word, and think about the context of the sentence. Write the number of the appropriate definition on the line next to the word. In addition, circle *noun, verb,* or *adjective* where indicated. Then choose the sentence with the correct answer.

1.

> **surface** *n.* **1** the outside layer of an object: *Rocks found on the beach usually have a smooth surface.* **2** the flat top level of s.t.: *the surface of a table (a pond, a mirror).* **3** outward appearance: *On the surface, that looks like a good car, but the engine is bad.* **4 to skim the surface:** to treat superficially: *The solution that you propose only skims the surface of the problem. -v.* **-faced, -facing, -faces 1** to rise to the surface: *We saw two whales surface and then dive back into the ocean.* **2** to appear: *That problem surfaced when our mechanic examined the car.* **3** to cover a road with asphalt or paving material: *They surfaced the new road last week.*

To understand what causes earthquakes, we need to understand the nature of the earth and the changes that are slowly taking place in the earth's **surface,** or crust, which is made of rock.

a. **surface:** _____ (noun / verb)

b. 1. We need to understand the nature of the earth and the changes that are slowly taking place in the outside layer of the earth.

   2. We need to understand the nature of the earth and the changes that are slowly taking place in the flat top level of the earth.

   3. We need to understand the nature of the earth and the changes that are slowly taking place in the outward appearance of the earth.

2.

> **strike** *v.* **struck, struck or stricken, strik-ing, strikes** **1** to hit hard: *She struck her brother and gave him a bloody nose.* || *The hammer struck the nail.* **2** to run into, *(syn.)* to **collide** with: *The car rolled down the hill and struck a tree.* **3** to attack: *The army struck by surprise at night.* **4** to happen or appear suddenly: *A good idea struck me as I was reading the newspaper.* **5** to have an effect on, to affect: *The power of her words struck me.* **6** to find suddenly, discover: *The workers will strike oil if they dig deep enough.* **7** to take away, *(syns.)* to **erase, eliminate:** *Strike the second paragraph, but leave the first and third.* **8** to stop working because of disagreements with management: *The bus drivers are striking until the owners give them more vacation time.* **9** to make fire or light by hitting or rubbing: *to strike a match;* **10** to make a note or sound: *He struck a C-sharp on the piano.* || *The clock is striking midnight.*

The Northridge earthquake **struck** the San Fernando Valley region of Southern California on January 17, 1994.

a. **strike:** _____

b. 1. The Northridge earthquake appeared suddenly in the San Fernando Valley region of Southern California on January 17, 1994.

   2. The Northridge earthquake ran into the San Fernando Valley region of Southern California on January 17, 1994.

   3. The Northridge earthquake hit the San Fernando Valley region of Southern California on January 17, 1994.

3.

> **fault** *n.* **1** an imperfection, *(syns.)* a **flaw**, **defect**: *There is a fault in the computer system.* **2** a weak point in s.o.'s character, *(syns.)* a **shortcoming, foible**: *He has some faults, such as sometimes talking too much.* **3** blame, responsibility (for a mistake): *Nobody knew who was at fault for the train accident.* **4** a large crack in the surface of the earth: *The San Andreas fault lies near San Francisco, where the fault line runs north and south.* **5 to a fault**: more than is necessary: *That man is careful in his business dealings to a fault.* **6 to find fault with**: to criticize usu. too often, *(syn.)* to **carp** about: *He complained that his boss was always finding fault with his work.*

The Kobe earthquake caused so much destruction because it produced a **fault** break directly through the business area of a city.

a. **fault:** ____

b. 1. The Kobe earthquake caused so much destruction because it produced an imperfection directly through the business area of a city.

   2. The Kobe earthquake is blamed for so much destruction because it produced a break directly through the business area of a city.

   3. The Kobe earthquake caused so much destruction because it produced a large crack in the earth's surface directly through the business area of a city.

4.

> **survive** *v.* **-vived, -viving, -vives 1** to continue to live or exist, esp. for a long time or under hard conditions, to endure: *This tree has survived for many years.* **2** to outlast adversity or a threat to existence: *She was lucky to survive the plane crash.*

People can reduce loss of life, injuries, and property damage by sufficiently preparing themselves, their homes, work places, and communities for a major earthquake. After all, it is possible to **survive** an earthquake.

a. **survive:** _____

b. 1. After all, it is possible to prepare for and endure an earthquake.

   2. After all, it is possible to prepare for and outlast an earthquake.

   3. After all, it is possible to threaten an earthquake.

PART 1

In English, some verbs become nouns by adding the suffix *-ment,* for example, *improve (v.), improvement (n.).* Complete each sentence with the correct form of the word on the left. **Write all the verbs in the simple present tense. They may be affirmative or negative. The nouns may be singular or plural.**

move *(v.)*
movement *(n.)*

1. a. The continents _____ on plates on the earth's crust.
   b. We don't notice the _____ because it is very slow.

place *(v.)*
placement *(n.)*

2. a. Schools usually _____ new students into different English classes depending on their English abilities.
   b. The students' _____ depend on the scores they get on an English test.

announce *(v.)*
announcement *(n.)*

3. a. Television stations interrupt programs to make important _____ as soon as they receive the news.
   b. However, the stations generally _____ small news items until the regular news programs.

measure *(v.)*
measurement *(n.)*

4. a. Many scientists _____ the intensity of an earthquake with a Richter scale.
   b. The Richter scale's _____ range from 1 to 10, where 10 is the most intense.

require *(v.)*
requirement *(n.)*

5. a. Most American colleges have an English _____ for foreign students.
   b. For instance, many colleges generally _____ a TOEFL score of 500 or higher.

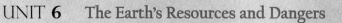

In English, the noun form and the verb form of some words are the same, for example, *cover (v.), cover (n.)*. Complete each sentence with the correct form of the word on the left. Circle (*v.*) if you are using the verb or (*n.*) if you are using the noun form of each word. **Write all the verbs in the simple present tense. They may be affirmative or negative. The nouns may be singular or plural.**

fear

1. a. Tom has a terrible _____ of airplanes.
        (v., n.)

    b. Tom _____ airplanes so much that he
            (v., n.)
        never even goes to airports.

change

2. a. People need to make many _____ when
                                    (v., n.)
        they move to another country.

    b. However, they _____ everything in their lives!
                        (v., n.)

break

3. a. The movement of the earth _____ many
                                    (v., n.)
        manmade objects that are underground, such as telephone and power lines, and gas and water pipelines.

    b. Any _____ in a gas line can cause dangerous
            (v., n.)
        fires wherever an earthquake occurs.

damage

4. a. Earthquakes of high intensity cause a lot of _____
        to buildings, roads, and bridges.   *(v., n.)*

    b. Earthquakes also _____ homes, dams,
                            (v., n.)
        and gas and water pipelines.

design

5. a. Eve has a book full of her own _____ for
                                        (v., n.)
        women's clothes.

    b. However, she is only interested in formal clothes. She
        _____ sports or casual clothes.
            (v., n.)

Read the earthquake survivor's story. Then answer the questions which follow.

A Survivor's Story

My name is Keiko Tanaka, and I live in Kobe, Japan. Because I was born and raised in Japan, I have experienced many earthquakes. By far the most powerful and frightening earthquake I have ever lived through was the one that struck my city on January 16, 1995.

My son's family and I live in a small house in Kobe. When the earthquake began, it was only 5:46 A.M. and we were all sleeping. I was thrown from my bed onto the carpet. I wanted to get to my son and his wife, but I couldn't—the amount of movement in our home was incredible. The door near where I was standing was swinging back and forth. I listened helplessly while just about everything standing in our home fell over. Loose objects were tossed across rooms, while the shaking continued. The noise was incredibly loud. When the earthquake finally stopped, I hurried to my son's room, where he, his wife Mika, and their children had been sleeping. Then we looked around our home. It had been heavily damaged. All the windows were broken, and the roof had fallen in. In the kitchen, most of the dishes lay in small pieces all across the kitchen floor. Outside, we saw that our neighbors' houses had fallen down, too. People were standing near their homes, and everyone looked shocked and frightened.

Although we were all safe and no one had been hurt, we were still very affected by a terrible fear. In addition, we did not have electrical power or water for days. Overall, it was a terrifying experience that we worry may happen again. In the meantime, we are all beginning to try to rebuild our homes and our lives. We love our beautiful city of Kobe and do not want to leave it.

QUESTIONS FOR ANOTHER LOOK

Read the survivor's story. Then answer the following questions.

1. The writer says that **"... because I was born and raised in Japan, I have experienced a lot of earthquakes."** This sentence tells us that
   a. the writer speaks Japanese
   b. Japan has a lot of earthquakes
   c. earthquakes are very frightening

2. Why was the noise **incredibly loud** during the earthquake?

   _____

   _____

3. What kind of damage did the Tanaka home have after the earthquake?

   _____

   _____

4. Do you think the Tanaka family will continue to live in Kobe? Why or why not?

   _____

   _____

1. A seismograph is an instrument that scientists use to locate and record earthquakes. Scientists measure the energy, or intensity, of earthquakes with a Richter scale. The Richter scale measures the intensity of earthquakes on a scale of 1 to 10.

   Read the following list of earthquakes around the world. Then mark the location of each earthquake on the map. Write the number next to the star that indicates the location of the earthquake.

WORLD EARTHQUAKE SITES

		Recent Earthquakes Around the World		
Date		**Location**	**Intensity on Richter Scale**	**Number of Deaths**
1.	5/70	Peru	7.8	67,000
2.	9/73	Yokohama, Japan	8.3	200,000
3.	2/76	Guatemala	7.5	23,000
4.	7/76	Tangshan, China	7.8	243,000
5.	8/76	The Philippines	8.0	6,500
6.	10/80	Algeria	7.3	5,000
7.	11/80	Southern Italy	7.0	3,100
8.	9/85	Mexico City	8.1	9,000
9.	12/88	Armenia	6.8	55,000
10.	6/90	Northern Iran	7.7	35,000
11.	3/92	Eastern Turkey	6.2	4,000
12.	9/93	Maharashtra, South India	6.3	9,748
13.	1/94	Northridge, California	6.8	61
14.	1/95	Kobe, Japan	7.2	5,502
15.	5/95	Sakhalin Island, Russia	7.5	1,989
16.	5/98	Afghanistan	6.9	5,000

2. a. Read the following checklist for home safety during an earthquake.
   1. Make sure that hanging lights are not above beds.
   2. Make sure that beds are not right below heavy mirrors.
   3. Make sure that beds are not right below framed pictures.
   4. Make sure that beds are not right below shelves with lots of objects that can fall.
   5. Make sure that beds are not next to large windows.
   6. Take all heavy objects off high shelves.
   7. Take all breakable objects off high shelves.
   8. Make sure that heavy mirrors are well fastened to walls.
   9. Make sure that heavy pictures are well fastened to walls.
   10. Make sure that air conditioners are well supported in windows.

   b. Look at the following bedroom. Refer to the checklist. In pairs or small groups, decide how to make the bedroom safer in the event of an earthquake. When you are finished, compare your safer bedroom with another group's bedroom.

3. It is important to know what to do during an earthquake. Read the following list. In pairs, decide what to do and what not to do during an earthquake. When you finish, compare your list with another pair of students. Be prepared to give reasons for your decisions.

___ Yes ___ No   a.   Stay calm and don't do anything to upset other people.

___ Yes ___ No   b.   Run to other rooms and shout, "Earthquake! Earthquake!"

___ Yes ___ No   c.   If you are indoors, get under a desk or a table, if possible.

___ Yes ___ No   d.   If you are in a high building, take the elevator to the first floor.

___ Yes ___ No   e.   If you are in a building, do not run outside. Falling objects are a danger.

___ Yes ___ No   f.   If you are outside near a building, stand in a doorway.

___ Yes ___ No   g.   If you are outside, but not near a building, try to get into an open area away from buildings and power lines.

___ Yes ___ No   h.   If you are in a car, continue driving to get as far away from the earthquake as possible.

___ Yes ___ No   i.   If the electrical power lines and gas lines break, use matches and candles for light.

___ Yes ___ No   j.   If you are in an empty room with no desk or table, stand in a doorway.

I. Topics FOR *Discussion* AND *Writing*

1. If you know someone who experienced an earthquake, interview that person. Then write a composition describing the person's experience.

2. Form a team of three. An earthquake took place an hour ago. Your team must organize a rescue in your school building. Decide what you have to do. List these actions in their order of importance. Assign responsibilities to each member of the team. Have each team member write a composition describing his or her plan of action.

3. Imagine that you are a teacher. Prepare a set of instructions for your students. Tell them what to do if an earthquake occurs.

4. **Write in your journal.** Imagine that an earthquake took place where you live. Describe the experience. What happened immediately before the earthquake? What happened during the earthquake? What happened after the earthquake? What did you think about? How did you feel?

Word Search

Read the words listed below. Find them in the puzzle and circle them. They may be written in any direction.

actual	earthquake	locate	predict
consider	furthermore	natural	resist
design	increase	occur	statistics

E R O M R E H T R U F Z S C L

S K Q R S I H L S D W V X L D

A L A R U T A N O S C W N A F

E U C U X L S O C C U R G P S

R N T R Q R T O E O A G I W O

C L U I K H A N K N B T S H Y

N G A E G D T P T S I S E R E

I G L Z F M I R D I Z C D H K

E E H C C H S E A D W W R Y Y

F A D L A Z T D I E Z X K T C

C M Z L L V I I F R V O E W N

J Y V K Z L C C K K S P X N R

O G U V S U S T C Q X K E S A

Read the clues on the next page. Write the answers in the correct spaces in the puzzle.

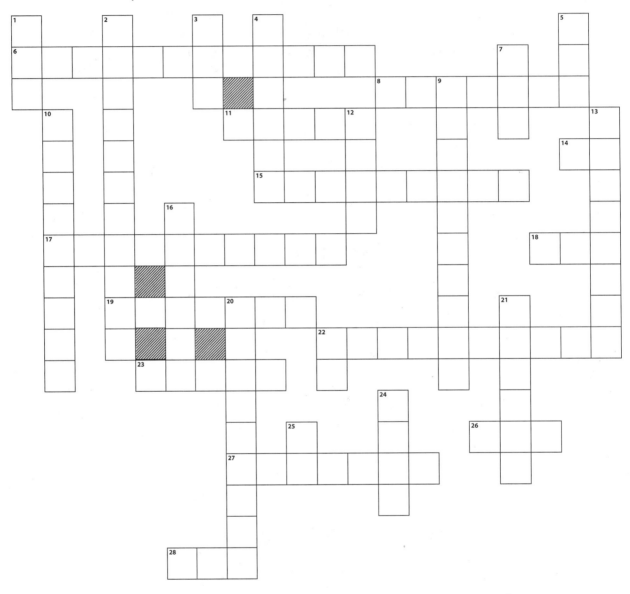

Crossword Puzzle Clues

Across Clues

6. Some small earthquakes are _____ , or unnoticeable.

8. I wanted coffee, but I drank tea _____.

11. The Tangshan earthquake _____ as the most deadly earthquake of all time.

14. We have class _____ Wednesday.

15. The Kobe earthquake cost an _____ $160 billion.

17. An _____ happens when the earth moves and the ground breaks up.

18. I have a birthday present _____ you.

19. Scientists cannot _____ the weather or earthquakes.

22. Dams, buildings, and bridges are _____.

23. Tell; say

26. Mark _____ swim very well.

27. Many people _____ earthquakes. Others do not; they are killed.

28. Scientists know _____ and how earthquakes happen. They don't know when.

Down Clues

1. The _____ is the star closest to the Earth.

2. A _____ is a machine for detecting earthquakes.

3. When an earthquake takes place, people need to _____ quickly to protect themselves.

4. Earthquakes cause a lot of _____ to buildings and roads.

5. The opposite of **subtract**

7. The opposite of **no**

9. The records of earthquake damage, deaths, and injuries are very frightening _____.

10. The number of earthquakes did not increase. The number _____.

12. The past tense of **slide**

13. Earthquakes kill some people, and cause _____ to other people.

16. The _____ of earthquakes is very high in some areas of the world.

20. The _____, or severity, of an earthquake is measured on a Richter scale.

21. The _____ of the Earth is called the crust.

22. Ann was tired, _____ she went to sleep.

24. I _____ a book about earthquakes. I bought it last week.

25. Scientists _____ trying to learn more about earthquakes.

L.

Grammar Cloze Quiz

Read the passage below. Complete each blank space with an article.

a	an	the

_____ (1) earth's crust is broken into _____ (2) number of large pieces called plates. _____ (3) continents ride on top of _____ (4) plates, and move with them. _____ (5) plates move very slowly, usually at _____ (6) rate of about _____ (7) inch per year.

_____ (8) plates move in different directions. _____ (9) difference in motion causes the rocks to break. This is _____ (10) earthquake. _____ (11) earthquake happens in different ways. In some areas of _____ (12) earth, _____ (13) plates move apart. This happens in _____ (14) middle of _____ (15) Atlantic Ocean. _____ (16) plates are sliding past one another in other regions of _____ (17) world, for example, at _____ (18) San Andreas fault zone in California. In other places, plates push directly against each other, and one plate moves downward under another plate. For example, _____ (19) plate is moving under another one off _____ (20) western coasts of South and Central America, and Japan.

The earth produces oil, which is very useful. The Earth also creates earthquakes, which are very destructive. Work with a classmate. Make a list of other things that the Earth produces which are very useful. Then make a list of other things that the Earth produces which are destructive. Explain your choices.

CNN V I D E O R E P O R T : Solar Roofs

1. In your opinion, what are some advantages of solar energy? What are some disadvantages?

2. Read these questions and then watch the video once or twice. Circle the letters of the correct answers.

    1. While Evelyn Ramsey is at work, her roof _____.
        a. generates electricity   b. gets very cool   c. turns red
    2. During the day the electric meter spins _____.
        a. forwards   b. backwards   c. upside down
    3. A solar roof for an average size house costs about _____ dollars.
        a. 250   b. 10,000   c. 15,000
    4. By reducing energy bills, the roof will pay for itself in _____ years.
        a. 5 to 10   b. 10 to 15   c. 15 to 20
    5. The state of California pays for _____ of the cost of a solar roof.
        a. one third   b. one half   c. two thirds

3. Discuss these questions with a partner or group: Would you like to live in a house with a solar roof? Why or why not?

Surfing THE INTERNET

Use a search engine, such as Netscape, Yahoo, Google, or Excite. Insert the key words: "alternative energy" and look for alternative energy sources besides solar energy. What are other kinds of alternative energy? Report what you discover to the class.

Optional activity: Read the article at http://www.millionsolarroofs.org/about_initiative about the Solar Roofs Initiative. How many solar roofs does the SRI hope to install by 2010? One type of solar technology is photovoltaic cells. What is the other type?

INDEX OF KEY WORDS AND PHRASES

SKILLS INDEX

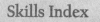